Scott Thornbury's 30 Language Teaching Methods

Cambridge Handbooks for Language Teachers

This series, now with over 50 titles, offers practical ideas, techniques and activities for the teaching of English and other languages, providing inspiration for both teachers and trainers.

The Pocket Editions come in a handy, pocket-sized format and are crammed full of tips and ideas from experienced English language teaching professionals, to enrich your teaching practice.

Recent titles in this series:

Grammar Practice Activities (Second edition)
A practical guide for teachers
PENNY UR

Vocabulary Activities
PENNY UR

Classroom Management Techniques
JIM SCRIVENER

CLIL Activities
A resource for subject and language teachers
LIZ DALE AND ROSIE TANNER

Language Learning with Technology
Ideas for integrating technology in the classroom
GRAHAM STANLEY

Translation and Own-language Activities
PHILIP KERR

Language Learning with Digital Video
BEN GOLDSTEIN AND PAUL DRIVER

Discussions and More
Oral fluency practice in the classroom
PENNY UR

Interaction Online
Creative Activities for Blended Learning
LINDSAY CLANDFIELD AND JILL HADFIELD

Activities for Very Young Learners
HERBERT PUCHTA AND KAREN ELLIOTT

Recent Pocket Editions:

Penny Ur's 100 Teaching Tips
PENNY UR

Jack C. Richards' 50 Tips for Teacher Development
JACK C. RICHARDS

Scott Thornbury's 30 Language Teaching Methods

Scott Thornbury

Consultant and editor: Philip Kerr

CAMBRIDGE
UNIVERSITY PRESS

University Printing House, Cambridge CB2 8BS, United Kingdom

One Liberty Plaza, 20th Floor, New York, NY 10006, USA

477 Williamstown Road, Port Melbourne, VIC 3207, Australia

314-321, 3rd Floor, Plot 3, Splendor Forum, Jasola District Centre, New Delhi - 110025, India

79 Anson Road, #06-04/06, Singapore 079906

Cambridge University Press is part of the University of Cambridge.

It furthers the University's mission by disseminating knowledge in the pursuit of education, learning and research at the highest international levels of excellence.

www.cambridge.org
Information on this title: www.cambridge.org/9781108408462

© Cambridge University Press 2017

First published 2017

20 19 18 17 16 15 14 13 12 11 10 9 8 7 6 5 4 3 2 1

A catalogue record for this publication is available from the British Library

ISBN 978-1-108-40846-2 Paperback
ISBN 978-1-108-40847-9 Apple iBook
ISBN 978-1-108-40848-6 Google ebook
ISBN 978-1-108-40849-3 Kindle ebook
ISBN 978-1-108-40850-9 eBooks.com ebook

Contents

Thanks

I owe a huge debt of gratitude to Philip Kerr, whose rigorous and insightful feedback kept me focused throughout the writing process, and to Alison Sharpe, equally vigilant, during the editing. And thanks to Karen Momber and Jo Timerick at Cambridge for their constant support and encouragement.

Scott Thornbury

Acknowledgements

The authors and publishers acknowledge the following sources of copyright material and are grateful for the permissions granted. While every effort has been made, it has not always been possible to identify the sources of all the material used, or to trace all copyright holders. If any omissions are brought to our notice, we will be happy to include the appropriate acknowledgements on reprinting and in the next update to the digital edition, as applicable.

Text

Cambridge University Press for the text on p. 2 from 'Reexamining the Critical Period Hypothesis: A Case Study of a Successful Adult SLA in a Naturalistic Environment' by Georgette Ioup, Elizabeth Boustagui, Manal El Tigi, and Martha Moselle in *Studies in Second Language Acquisition*, Vol. 16 (01), p. 77. Copyright © 1994 Cambridge University Press; National Geographic Society for the text on p. 4 from 'Don Francisco's Six Steps to Better English' in *How I Learned English: 55 Accomplished Latinos Recall Lessons in Language and Life* by Tom Miller. Copyright © 2007 National Geographic Society; Graham Greene for the text on p. 10 from *The Confidential Agent* by Graham Greene, published by Penguin Books Ltd. Copyright © 1939, 1971 Graham Greene. Rosetta Stone Ltd. for the text on p. 11 from 'Learn Languages: Rosetta Stone', https://play.google.com/store/apps/details?id=air.com.rosettastone.mobile.CoursePlayer&hl=en. Copyright © Rosetta Stone Ltd. Reproduced with kind permission; The University of Chicago Press for the text on p. 13 from *Teaching Foreign-Language Skills* by Wilga M. Rivers. Copyright © 1968, 1981 The University of Chicago Press. John Wiley & Sons Inc. for the text on p. 19 from 'The Reading Approach and The New Method System' by Michael West, *The Modern Language Journal*, Vol 22. (03), pp. 220–222. Copyright © 1937 John Wiley & Sons Inc. Reproduced with permission of John Wiley & Sons Inc. granted via the Copyright Clearance Center; The University of Michigan Press for the text on p. 23 and p. 24 from *English Pattern Practices: Establishing the Patterns as Habits* by Robert Lado and Charles C. Fries. Copyright © 1943, 1970 The University of Michigan Press; Robert M. Ramsey for the text on p. 24 from *English Through Patterns* by Robert M. Ramsey, published by Editorial Teide S.A. Copyright © 1969 Robert M. Ramsey; Taylor and Francis for the text on p. 36 from *Foundations of Foreign Language Teaching: Nineteenth-Century Innovators*, Volume 1 by A.P.R. Howatt and Richard C. Smith. Copyright © 2000 Routledge, a Taylor and Francis imprint; Helbling Languages for the text on p. 45 from *Teaching Chunks of Language: From Noticing to Remembering* by Seth Lindstromberg and Frank Boers. Copyright © 2008 Helbling Languages. Reproduced with kind permission; Deakin University for the text on p. 47 from *Linguistic Processes in Sociolinguistic Practice* by Gunther R. Kress. Copyright © 1985 Deakin University Press; T. F. Mitchell for the text on p. 48 from *The Language of Buying and Selling in Cyrenaica:*

A *Situational Statement* reproduced in *Principles of Firthian Linguistics* by T. F. Mitchell. Copyright © 1975 Longman; The University of Michigan Press for the text on p. 51 from *Linguistics across Cultures: Applied Linguistics for Language Teachers* by Robert Lado. Copyright © 1957, 1971 The University of Michigan Press; Oxford University Press for the text on pp. 57–58 from *English in Situations* by Robert O'Neill. Copyright © 1970 Oxford University Press. Reproduced with permission; Oxford University Press for the text on p. 58 from *English in Situations* by Robert O'Neill. Copyright © 1970 Oxford University Press; Brian Abbs and Ingrid Freebairn for the text on p. 61 from *Building Strategies: Teacher's Book* by Brian Abbs and Ingrid Freebairn, published by Longman. Copyright © 1984 Brian Abbs and Ingrid Freebairn. Reproduced with kind permission; Cambridge University Press for the text on p. 62 from *Touchstone 1 Teacher's Edition* by Michael McCarthy, Jeanne McCarten and Helen Sandiford Copyright © 2005 Cambridge University Press. Reproduced with kind permission; Council of Europe for the text on p. 69 from *Common European Framework of Reference for Languages: Learning, Teaching, Assessment.* Copyright © Council of Europe. Reproduced with kind permission; Marie Wilson Nelson for the text on p. 74 from *At the Point of Need: Teaching Basic and ESL Writers* by Marie Wilson Nelson, published by Heinemann, a division of Houghton Mifflin Harcourt. Copyright © 1991 Marie Wilson Nelson. Reproduced with kind permission; Delta Publishing for the text on p. 82 from *Teaching Unplugged: Dogme in English Language Teaching* by Luke Meddings and Scott Thornbury. Copyright © 2009 Delta Publishing. Reproduced with kind permission; University of Alberta for the text on p. 85 from *Language, Consciousness and Personal Growth: An Autobiographic Study of a Second Language Learner* by Zhou Wu. Copyright © 1993 University of Alberta. Reproduced with kind permission; Natural News for the text on p. 90 from 'The Top Ten Technologies: #10 Superlearning Systems' by Mike Adams, Natural News website, 14.07.2014. Copyright © 2014 Natural News; Da Capo Press for the text on p. 95 from *How Children Fail* by John Holt. Copyright © 1982 Da Capo Press, a Hachette Book Group Company; Oxford University Press for the text on p. 96 from *The Multilingual Subject* by Claire J. Kramsch. Copyright © 2009 Oxford University Press; Trustees of Dartmouth College for the text on p. 99 from 'The Method' http://rassias.dartmouth. edu/method/. Copyright © 2017 Trustees of Dartmouth College. Reproduced with kind permission; Condé Nast for the text on p. 99 from 'Crazy English: The National Scramble to Learn a New Language Before the Olympics' by Evans Osnos, The New Yorker website, 28.04.2008. Copyright © 2008 Condé Nast; The Mezzofanti Guild for the text on p. 119 from 'You Don't Need to Study Grammar to Learn a Foreign Language' by Donovan Nagel. Copyright © The Mezzofanti Guild; Lindsay Does Languages by 'Why Social Media is the Best Free Language Learning Tool', Lindsay Does Languages website, 15.11.2016. Copyright © 2016 Lindsay Does Languages; HarperCollins for the text on 119 from *Fluent in 3 Months: Tips and Techniques to Help You Learn Any Language* by Benny Lewis. Copyright © 2014 HarperCollins; Alexander Arguelles for the text on p. 120 from 'Foreign Language Expertise', http://www.foreignlanguageexpertise.com/about.html. Copyright © 2011 Alexander Arguelles; Speaking Fluently for the text on p. 120 from 'The Secret of Learning Languages' by Richard Simcott, Speaking Fluently website, 11.02.2016. Copyright © 2016 Speaking Fluently.

Why I wrote this book

'Another book about methods? I thought methods were dead. I thought we were now in a post-method era.'

It's true that the concept of 'method' is generally shunned in the literature on language teaching nowadays. Even as long ago as 1969, L.G. Kelly, in his survey of language teaching over the last 25 centuries, contended that 'methods are of little interest'. In similar fashion, H. H. Stern (1983) announced 'a break with the method concept', due in part to the failure of researchers to find any significant advantage in one method over another. In 1990, N.S. Prabhu wrote an influential paper called 'There is no best method – why?' and in the following year Dick Allwright published another called 'The Death of Method'.

Subsequently, B. Kumaravadivelu (1994) identified what he called the 'postmethod condition', a result of 'the widespread dissatisfaction with the conventional concept of method'. At around the same time, Adrian Holliday (1994) was arguing the case for 'appropriate methodology' which must, first and foremost, be sensitive to the local culture – something which imported methods are probably not.

Nevertheless, in the popular imagination at least, faith in the idea of method persists. Websites advertising new and improved methods for language learning abound. Here are some promotional slogans taken at random:

> Learning a foreign language is easy with the XXX Method.
> The highly acclaimed YYY Method lets you pick up a new language naturally.
> Over a period of more than 15 years, ZZZ has developed and perfected a unique method of teaching languages.

What's more, training courses regularly include a component on the history of language teaching methods. Teachers in general are intrigued by the variety of methods that have been proposed, and are often keen to experiment with them. Indeed, as D. Bell (2007) discovered, when he canvassed a number of teachers, 'methods, however the term is defined, are not dead. Teachers seem to be aware of both the usefulness of methods and the need to go beyond them'.

One attraction of methods is that they offer coherent templates for generating classroom routines. The method helps structure what – to both teachers and learners – is a potentially haphazard experience. It provides answers to questions like: *Where do I start? What materials and activities should I use? In what order? To what end?* For novice teachers, in particular, methods offer a lifeline. For more experienced teachers, they offer a toolkit. As Richards and Rodgers (2014) put it, 'methods can be studied not as prescriptions for how to teach but as a source of well-used practices, which teachers can adapt or implement based on their own needs'.

Of course, a method is of not much use if we don't believe in it – if, in Prabhu's (1990) terms, it contravenes a teacher's 'sense of plausibility'. Methods are underpinned by beliefs about learning and language and, even if these are not always made explicit, we need to feel in harmony with them.

But if the method does fit, if it does resonate with our beliefs, then it has every chance of working – not because it is intrinsically sound (remember 'there is no best method'), but because it confers on a teacher a degree of confidence in his or her own efficacy. Jane Spiro (2013) puts it very well: 'The critical factor in success is the commitment and belief of the teacher in the methods he or she is using, and the continuing reflection of the teacher as to whether these methods are making a positive difference'.

This book, then, aims to unpack – not just the history of methods – but the beliefs that underpin them and the benefits that still might possibly accrue from experimenting with them.

Some notes on terminology

Not all the methods included in this book have *method* as part of their label: some are called *approaches*, and one is simply a *way*. But they are all consistent with David Nunan's (2003) definition: 'A language teaching method is a single set of procedures which teachers are to follow in the classroom. Methods are usually based on a set of beliefs about the nature of language and learning'. Researchers are quick to point out, of course, that no two teachers will implement a method in exactly the same way – hence the idea of a method being 'a single set of procedures' is necessarily an idealized one. For this reason, I am ignoring the distinction that is often made between *method* and *approach*, because, in terms of what happens in actual classrooms, it is of little consequence.

Methodology, on the other hand, is a more general term to characterize the classroom procedures and activities that teachers select – such as error correction, group work, or video viewing – and the way that these are managed, irrespective of the specific method that they subscribe to.

How this book is organized

Most training courses and methodology texts include a section on 'the history of methods' and this typically takes the form of a 'modernist' narrative, i.e. one of uninterrupted progress from 'darkness into light'. In actual fact, a closer reading of the history suggests that this account is over-simplified, and that methods not only co-exist, often for long periods of time, but are continuously re-invented out of the same basic ingredients. This book, then, aims to counteract the traditional narrative by grouping methods according to what they have in common, even if separated in time, and to dispel the view that methods 'die' and no longer have anything to offer us.

The choice of methods to include has been motivated by a number of factors: primarily, the strength of their influence over time (e.g. the Direct Method, Communicative Language Teaching), but, conversely, their relative failure to gain wider acceptance, despite their intrinsic merits (e.g. the Comparative Method, text memorization). Rehabilitating these 'lost methods' because of what they still might have to offer us has been another reason I wrote this book. Also included are those ways in which people learn languages that are not classroom-based, thereby stretching Nunan's definition (above) to extend to self-study and even immersion. At the same time, this book does not hope to be exhaustive, neither in terms of the methods that it covers nor in terms of the detail with which each one is described. Space simply does not permit.

Despite these limitations, it is hoped that you will not only have a broader understanding of the enormous variety of ways that languages are – and have been – learned, but also be in a better position to evaluate some current practices – a necessary step in our continued professional development.

Abbreviations

To save space, and repetition, here is a list of common abbreviations used in this book:

EFL = English as a foreign language

ELF = English as a lingua franca

ESL = English as a second language

ELT = English language teaching

L1 = first language/mother tongue
L2 = second (or additional) language

SLA = second language acquisition

TESOL = teaching English to speakers of other languages

Bell, D. (2007) Do teachers think that methods are dead? *ELT Journal*, 61: 135–143.

Holliday, A. (1994) *Appropriate Methodology and Social Context*. Cambridge: Cambridge University Press.

Kelly, L.G. (1969) *25 Centuries of Language Teaching: 500 BC – 1969*. Rowley, MA: Newbury House.

Kumaravadivelu, B. (1994) The Postmethod condition: (E)merging strategies for second/ foreign language teaching. *TESOL Quarterly*, 28: 27–48.

Nunan, D. (ed.) (2003) *Practical English Language Teaching*. New York: McGraw-Hill.

Prabhu, N.S. (1990) There is no best method – why? *TESOL Quarterly*, 24:161–176.

Richards, J. C. and Rodgers, T.S. (2014) *Approaches and Methods in Language Teaching (3rd edition)*. Cambridge: Cambridge University Press.

Spiro, J. (2013) *Changing Methodologies in TESOL*. Edinburgh: Edinburgh University Press.

Stern, H.H. (1983) *Fundamental Concepts of Language Teaching*. Oxford: Oxford University Press.

A: Natural methods

This first section looks at a number of methods that are loosely characterized as being 'natural' – in the sense that they replicate, or aim to replicate – the processes by which first languages are acquired, or by which second languages are picked up without any formal instruction.

1 Total Immersion

What more natural way of learning an additional language than immersing yourself in the culture that speaks it? It is also the most widely practised way: more people have acquired a language through total immersion than by any other means.

The background

It may seem odd to begin a book on methods with a 'zero-method'. After all, total immersion pre-dates the concept of 'method' by several hundreds of millennia. Ever since people first moved – or were forced to move – away from their local speech community, they have come into contact with other languages. And, given time and motivation, they have learned them – often to impressive levels of ability. Hence, total immersion supplies the benchmark against which the success of all other methods can be measured.

Take 'Julie', for instance. Julie was a British woman who married an Egyptian and settled in Cairo aged 21. She never attended classes in Egyptian Arabic, and could not read or write in it, but within just two and a half years she was able to 'pass' as a native speaker of the language. How was she able to achieve this? Probably because she was totally immersed in Arabic. As the researchers who studied her (Ioup et al 1994) describe it:

> Nine days after arrival, her husband was unexpectedly called to military service and she was left with non-speaking-English relatives for 45 days. Since there was no one to assist her in English, she relied on context and gesture to interpret utterances and express meaning. Thus, at this initial stage her language acquisition situation resembled the environment for child L1 acquisition.

By the time her husband returned she was able to communicate with her in-laws using simple sentences and idiomatic expressions and, after six months, she was fairly fluent. The immersion process continued when she took a job in an Egyptian school, and, after three years in Egypt, she no longer used English with her husband or children: Arabic had, effectively, become the home language (although her children did grow up bilingual).

Julie's case is only exceptional in that, despite being a late starter, she achieved a degree of proficiency in her second language that is relatively unusual in adults. But the situation of being suddenly immersed in a language and having to pick it up 'naturalistically' is one that is familiar to most immigrants, even if they don't always 'pass' as native speakers. And, while it may be arguable whether immersion is a 'method' as such, there is a widespread view – supported by stories such as Julie's – that, if you have to learn a second language, then the best thing you can do is hop on a plane and go to the country where the language is spoken. Many 'off the shelf' methods, such as the **Natural Method** (see chapter **2**), in fact, attempt to simulate the immersion experience.

Of course, not all naturalistic (i.e. non-instructed) learners are successful. In another seminal case study of an immigrant's command of English, 'Alberto', an adult Costa Rican who had been living in Boston for a year and a half, was incapable of producing anything more than very basic ('pidginized') English. This was attributed to his lack of integration into the dominant English-speaking culture. Conversely, in another case study (Schmidt 1983), an adult Japanese immigrant ('Wes') living in Hawaii, who was seemingly well integrated, also showed little language development over the three years he was studied. He did, however, achieve impressive levels of communicative effectiveness, such that many who knew him rated his English favourably. (English teachers, on the other hand, were less impressed!)

How does it work?

Total immersion on its own seems to be less effective than total immersion *plus*. That is to say, as well as round-the-clock exposure, there needs to be some 'push' for greater precision, and there needs to be some focused attention on form. (It's probably the lack of both that accounts for the limited language development in the case of both Alberto and Wes.)

For example, to help her cope with the initial experience of total immersion, Julie kept a notebook in which she jotted down any words or expressions she could make sense of. She started to include grammatical information, such as verb endings, too. But, at this initial stage, of most use were formulaic 'chunks', which gave her a toe-hold into real communication. She also took (grateful) note of the corrections and re-phrasings that her relatives offered her when communication broke down.

In similar vein, another self-taught learner, the Chilean Marcos Kreutzberger (better known as the TV personality Don Francisco) devised a number of proactive strategies for learning English when he was 'immersed' in New York, aged 19. On the streets of the city, for example, he would seek out 'older people who didn't seem to be in a hurry', and, on the pretext of asking directions, initiate a conversation. He would write down any new words that might come up in a personal lexicon for later recycling. He supplemented this routine by watching TV, reading newspapers 'and trying to translate everything that was going on' (Kreutzberger 2007). He adds:

> The system really worked for me. After 90 days I could navigate pretty well, and after a year I felt I had enough ability to join in conversations and understand almost everything being said.

Does it work?

For Julie and Marcos, immersion was clearly successful. For Wes less so, and for Alberto hardly at all. What made the difference? As mentioned, the use of deliberate strategies to filter and record the input, to pay attention to corrections, and to plan subsequent exchanges, all seemed to play an important part in the success of Julie and Marcos. Just as important may have been their willingness to take risks, which, in turn, may have been driven by sheer necessity: in Julie's case in particular, she had no choice but to learn Arabic.

Of course, Julie and Marcos were successful *speakers* of their target languages. But we don't know a lot about their reading and writing skills. Whereas total immersion can lead to very high levels of proficiency in oracy (speaking and listening), literacy skills typically lag behind. This is because, outside of an academic context, learners simply don't get the exposure to written text, or the practice producing it, that literacy requires.

What's in it for us?

The idea that classroom instruction can be adapted so as to replicate the conditions of total immersion is a seductive, but ultimately doomed, one. For a start, we have seen that only highly motivated and resourceful learners may truly benefit from a total immersion experience. More realistically, it is virtually impossible to recreate the all day, every day quantity of exposure that total immersion provides. On the other hand, technological innovations have exponentially increased contact opportunities outside the classroom. Training learners in the strategies that enable them to take advantage of these opportunities may be one way forward. These could include using online means to interact with speakers of the target language through websites such as 'HelloTalk' (www.hellotalk.com), for example.

Ioup, G., Boustagoui, E., Tigi, M., & Moselle, M. (1994) Reexamining the critical period hypothesis: a case of a successful adult SLA in a naturalistic environment. *Studies in SLA*, 16: 73–98.

Kreutzberger, M. (2007) Don Francisco's Six Steps to Better English. In Miller, T. (ed.) *How I learned English*, Washington, DC: National Geographic.

Schmidt, R. (1983) Interaction, acculturation and the acquisition of communicative competence. In Wolfson, N., & Judd, E. (eds.) *Sociolinguistics and Second Language Acquisition*. Rowley, Mass.: Newbury House.

2 The Natural Method/Approach

Total immersion works because, like first language acquisition, it is 'natural'. That, at least, is the argument made by proponents of the so-called natural methods.

The background

It's fair to say that the history of language teaching has swung back and forth between just two poles. On the one hand, there have been methods that take the position that additional languages have to be *learned* – through the application of some kind of mental effort. This is because additional languages are not picked up on our mother's knee, as it were. At the other extreme are the methods that are grounded in the belief that, given the right conditions, additional languages *can* be acquired in the same way we acquired our mother tongue. Because they attempt to replicate at least some of the conditions of uninstructed acquisition, these latter methods are loosely grouped together as 'natural methods'. Over time, one or two have explicitly labelled themselves as being the Natural Method, or the Natural Approach.

Perhaps the strongest argument supporting natural approaches is not that we learned our first language naturally, but that many, many people have learned a second language naturally – that is, without formal instruction but solely through contact with speakers of the language – in a manner often referred to as naturalistic learning (see chapter **1 Immersion**). For early scholars, naturalistic learning was equated to 'learning through conversation'. As the enlightenment philosopher John Locke put it, in *Some Thoughts Concerning Education* (1693): 'The Original way of Learning a language by Conversation, not only serves well enough, but is to be prefer'd as the most Expedite, Proper, and Natural'.

One of the first attempts to formalize such a philosophy for the teaching of modern languages was instituted by a teacher of French. In a book called *Causeries avec mes élèves* (*Conversations with my students*, 1874a), Lambert Sauveur describes the first lesson: 'It is a conversation during two hours *in the French language* with twenty persons who know nothing of this language. After five minutes only, I am carrying on a dialogue with them, and this dialogue does not cease'. Sauveur opened a language school in Boston and before long his conversation-based method had attracted a great deal of attention and became known as the Natural Method.

Almost exactly a century later, Tracy Terrell, a teacher of Spanish in California, proposed a 'natural approach' to teaching second languages. Drawing on the distinction made by Stephen Krashen between *learning* (i.e. conscious study), on the one hand, and, on the other, *acquisition* (i.e. unconscious 'absorption' of the language through exposure and use), Terrell argued that communicative competence could be achieved in the classroom, not through learning-type activities, but through activities that fostered 'natural' acquisition. Such activities would be *communicative*, in that the focus would be entirely on meaning – initially simply understanding meaningful input, and then producing meaningful output. Perhaps more firmly grounded in research than Sauveur's method, the Natural Approach nevertheless shares many of its basic principles.

How does it work?

In his *Introduction to the Teaching of Living Languages Without Grammar or Dictionary* (1874b), Sauveur explains the principle underpinning his 'conversations':

> I raise quickly my finger before you, and show it to you. Do you not understand, whatever your language may be, that that means *there is the finger*? And if I point my extended forefinger towards the table or the door, do you not understand that I say, *There is the table; there is the door*? And if, on showing you the finger, I say in my French language *Voilà le doigt* , do you not understand that the French pronounce these words to indicate that thing?

Simply by extending this idea almost indefinitely, Sauveur was able to weave conversations out of the 'here-and-now', with the learners responding minimally at first, but participating more fully as they became familiar with the material. The ultimate aim was that the learners would be able to interact with one another with minimal reliance on the teacher. Although the conversations were available in print form, Sauveur discouraged teachers from using the book in class: 'Give the pupils the book to read at home as preparation for your teaching, but forbid them to open it in the class; their ear alone must be occupied there'.

In similar fashion, Terrell's approach involves exposing learners to 'comprehensible input', e.g. in the form of commands (see chapter 7 **Total Physical Response**) and question-and-answer routines using real objects or visuals, to which the learners (unlike Sauveur's learners) are allowed to respond using their L1. Production is withheld until learners feel ready, and grammar explanation and error correction (being associated with learning and not with acquisition) are discouraged. Activities likely to cause stress or anxiety are also avoided, since, according to Terrell (1977) 'affective (not cognitive) factors are primary forces operating in language acquisition'.

Does it work?

Apart from the attention that Sauveur's method attracted at the time, its effectiveness was not really put to the test: we only have his word for it. He reports, for example, a class whose conversation, after four and a half months of five two-hour lessons a week, was 'so animated and so interesting' that, listening to them, he thought he was back in France. Certainly, compared to the prevailing grammar-translation methodology of the time, his Natural Method must have been a breath of fresh air. So, too, in its own way, was Terrell's Natural Approach, contrasting as it did with the forced production and rigorous correction associated with audiolingualism. However, in its outright rejection of learning-type classroom procedures, such as error correction, the Natural Approach might have let the pendulum swing too far in the direction of acquisition. The classroom, after all, is not a 'natural' context for language learning: apart from anything else, the amount of real exposure and practice that individual learners get is inevitably limited. At best, so-called natural approaches might serve as a relatively stress-free introduction to a language, after which more conventional methods might take over.

What's in it for us?

Despite those caveats, there is a lot to be learned from natural acquisition, whether of the first language or of an additional one. Basing language learning on 'conversations' (however we define these) makes a certain sense. As a number of researchers have observed, the grammar of first language acquisition *emerges* out of the conversations that the child has with his or her caregivers. Grammar is not a prerequisite for these conversations. It follows, therefore, that an approach to second language learning that foregrounds conversation might provide a fertile environment for the emergence of the second language grammar – especially if the conversations are 'enhanced' with explicit attention to the formal features of the language. So-called 'instructional conversations' are central to approaches that view learning as socially constructed, and mediated by talk – 'so that the knowledge that is created carries with it echoes of the conversations in which it was generated' (Mercer 1995).

Mercer, N. (1995) *The Guided Construction of Knowledge*. Clevedon: Multilingual Matters.

Sauveur, L. (1874a) *Causeries avec mes élèves*. Boston: Schoenhof and Moeller.

Sauveur, L. (1874b) *Introduction to the Teaching of Living Languages Without Grammar or Dictionary*. Boston: Schoenhof and Moeller.

Terrell, T. (1977) A natural approach to second language acquisition and learning. *Modern Language Journal*, 61: 325–336.

3 The Direct Method

'What is the method ... that I allude to?' asked Otto Jesperson in 1904, in attempting to pin down the way that the Reform Movement had transformed language teaching. 'The method is by some called the "new" or "newer"; ... by others the "reform-method," again the "natural," the "rational," the "correct," or "sensible" ...; the "direct" comes a little nearer... .' In fact, it was the 'direct' that stuck.

The background

In *The Confidential Agent* by Graham Greene (1939), the agent of the title, known simply as D., has to make contact with another spy, Mr K., who works in a language school in London. Mr K. teaches Entrenationo – an invented language like Esperanto. The director of the school, Dr Bellows, welcomes D. before taking him to his private lesson with Mr K. On the way, Bellows warns D.: 'We teach by the direct method. We trust – to your honour – not to speak anything but Entrenationo'. This is confirmed by Mr K. when the lesson starts: while loudly teaching words from a wall-chart and numbers using wooden blocks, he whispers: 'We are forbidden by the rules to talk anything but Entrenationo. I am fined one shilling if I am caught'. This, of course, makes the exchange of secrets with K. somewhat difficult, especially since Dr Bellows periodically enters the room to check that the rules are being followed.

As exaggerated as this scene is, it does capture the flavour of the Direct Method in its heyday, especially as practised by large language teaching franchises, such as the Berlitz chain. Maximilian Berlitz is, of course, the name that is indelibly associated with the Direct Method: he opened his first school in Providence, Rhode Island, in 1878, and, at the time that Greene was writing *The Confidential Agent*, there were Berlitz schools in most major cities in Europe and the Americas.

Berlitz was the first to mass-market the Direct Method, but he was by no means the first to argue that second language learning should be taught 'directly', i.e. unmediated by translation. The Reform Movement of the late nineteenth century provided the intellectual climate out of which a number of methods, including Berlitz's, emerged. All had in common a focus on teaching the spoken language, and on teaching it entirely in the L2. Early reformers – such as Lambert Sauveur (see chapter 2 **The Natural Method/Approach**) – had looked to first language acquisition for their inspiration. In the same fashion, Berlitz claimed that 'the Berlitz Method is the systematized application of the psychological laws which enable a child to learn its mother tongue' (1911/1917). These psychological laws took the form of what was called 'associationism' – the theory that language learning is essentially the forming and strengthening of associations between language items and their referents in the real world. As Henry Sweet (1899/1964) put it, 'the whole process of learning a language is one of forming associations'. Translation into or out of another language, on the other hand, might cause 'cross-associations', which interfere with the more direct links on which accurate and fluent production depends.

The view that learning a second language should replicate first language learning, and that it results from forming tight associations that are 'uncorrupted' by translation, is a core tenet of a number of mass-marketed online courses, such as Rosetta Stone:

> Learn a new language the way you learned your first. Fun, intuitive, immersive lessons teach you to speak and think in your new language. Develop fundamental language skills naturally with no translation or memorization required!

How does it work?

In Berlitz's schools, teaching was based on two 'fundamental principles' which he spelled out in the preface to his *First Book* (1911 edition):

1. Direct association of Perception and Thought with the Foreign Speech and Sound.
2. Constant and exclusive use of the Foreign Language.

Like Sauveur, Berlitz based his lessons – especially at elementary stages – around question-and-answer routines, using the objects and people in the here-and-now:

> I am writing on the blackboard. What am I doing? What am I writing on the blackboard? I am reading a book. What am I doing? What am I reading? Who is reading?

> I write letters; I write words; I write a sentence. What is this, a word or a letter? How many letters are there in the word *table?* How many words are there in this sentence? Etc.

Other features that characterize the Direct Method are the use of visual aids and real objects that substitute the need to use translation. The wall-chart described in *The Confidential Agent* is typical of its time: 'A family sat eating in front of what looked like a Swiss chalet. The father had a gun, and one lady an umbrella; there were mountains, forests, waterfalls; the table was crammed with an odd mixture of food – apples, and uncooked cabbage, a chicken, pears, oranges and raw potatoes, a joint of meat. A child played with a hoop, and a baby sat up in a pram drinking out of a bottle'.

Does it work?

There are few better accounts of experiencing the Direct Method first-hand than that of the linguist Roger Brown's attempt to learn Japanese at a Berlitz school in the 1970s (Brown 1973). It starts: 'My skilled and charming teacher began with the words: "How do you do? That's the last English we will use." And it was'. As a researcher of first language acquisition, Brown is particularly interested in the claim that the Direct Method replicates the experience of children acquiring their mother tongue – but he is sceptical:

> Working only in the new language can be a great strain on both teacher and student. Sometimes I think it really does lead to experiences akin to those of the preliterate child but often, surely not. […] The insistence on avoiding the first language sometimes seems to lead to a great waste of time and to problems children [learning their first language], for some reason, seem not to have. One long morning my teacher tried to put across three verbs, *kimasu, yukimasu*, and *kaerimasu*, with the aid

of paper and pencil drawings of pathways and persons and loci, and by much moving of herself and of me – uncomprehendingly passive as a patient in a hospital. But I could not grasp the concepts. I feel Mr Berlitz would have suffered no great dishonour if she had said to me that the concepts in question sometimes go by the names *come, go,* and *return.*

What's in it for us?

Despite Brown's misgivings, there is a lot to be said for maximising the use – by both teacher and learners – of the target language, and for discouraging an over-reliance on translation. Sustaining a monolingual lesson with elementary learners requires considerable inventiveness, and, if done well, can be immensely motivating. But withholding the use of the learners' L1 simply through a dogged faith in Berlitz's fundamental principles may be counterproductive. For this reason, some scholars (e.g. Wilga Rivers 1981) have argued for a 'modified' form of the Direct Method in which:

> teachers have reintroduced some grammatical explanations of a strictly functional kind, given in the native language, while retaining the inductive approach wherever possible. [...] They have also reintroduced occasional translation of words and phrases as a check on comprehension.

Berlitz, M. (1911/1917) *Method for Teaching Modern Languages. First Book (revised American edition)*. New York: Berlitz.

Brown, R. (1973) *A First Language: The Early Stages*. Cambridge, Mass.: Harvard University Press.

Jespersen, O. (1904) *How to Teach a Foreign Language*. London: George Allen & Unwin.

Rivers, W. (1981) *Teaching Foreign-Language Skills (2nd Edition)*. Chicago: University of Chicago Press.

Rosetta Stone: https://play.google.com/store/apps/details?id=air.com.rosettastone.mobile. CoursePlayer&hl=en

Sweet, H. (1899/1964) *The Practical Study of Languages*. Oxford: Oxford University Press.

4 The Oral Method

> 'The Oral Method will re-awaken and re-educate those spontaneous capacities for language study which are inherent in the human race; those innate powers manifested in the earliest years of childhood ...' (Palmer 1921a).

The background

In 1902, a 24-year- old Englishman from Hythe in Kent moved to Verviers in Belgium where he started teaching English – with no previous experience or training – in a Berlitz-type school. Like many before and after, he was captivated by the method that was practised (see chapter **3 The Direct Method**), and, within a year or two, he felt confident enough to go it alone and set up his own language school in the same town. His name was Harold Palmer, and he called the school the Palmer School and his variant on Berlitz's direct method he called the Palmer Method. Soon, not only English was being taught in his school but also German, Spanish and even Esperanto. Twenty years later, the insights into learning and teaching that he had gained in those formative years in Verviers were condensed into two books: *The Oral Method of Teaching Languages* (1921a) and *The Principles of Language Study* (1921b).

How does it work?

The principle underlying Palmer's approach is that 'language-study is essentially a habit-forming process' (1921b) and that learners need first to be trained to draw on their innate capacities for learning to ensure that the habits that are formed are good ones, not bad ones. This requires, among other things, learning to listen, i.e. an initial focus on receptive skills. So, although its name suggests that – like other natural approaches – the Oral Method prioritizes speaking, Palmer recognized the need for a purely receptive stage: an 'incubation' period which 'consists simply in the teacher's talking to the students in that language which is the object of study' (1921a), while ensuring, through his or her actions, that the talk is comprehensible:

> I'm touching the table – the floor – the chair. I'm going to touch the ceiling. I can't. I can't touch the ceiling; it's too high. I can touch the blackboard easily because it isn't too high … etc.

Students are not expected to respond in any way to this 'shower' of language: 'Their only efforts should be devoted to making out the general sense of what is being said'. 'Exercises in conscious oral assimilation,' on the other hand, involve listening activities that require the learners to focus their attention, and to respond non-verbally. This might include what Palmer called 'imperative drill' (what is now better known as **Total Physical Response**, see chapter 7), in which learners physically respond to commands from their teacher. But in all reading and listening work, the learner must be clear on the meaning of the content. For Palmer, there were four ways of presenting meaning: by direct association with the thing itself (as in 'This is a book'); by translation (and, unlike other, stricter direct method practitioners, Palmer considered translation 'perfectly harmless and in many cases positively beneficial' (1921b); by definition; and through contextualization. For Palmer, exemplification was worth any number of rules: 'A well-chosen example or set of examples may so completely embody the rule that the rule itself will be superfluous' (1921b).

Oral production activities involve simple imitation initially, on the grounds that until a word or phrase is articulated, it is not remembered, and if it is not remembered, it is not learned. Articulation need not be out loud, though: subvocalization (repeating under your breath) was considered sufficient. What follows the imitation stage is a succession of drill-type activities, involving learners responding orally to different kinds of prompts from the teacher. The object is always to 'fix' the target items in memory. These 'conventional conversations', as Palmer called them, must be conducted at speed, so as to ensure 'automatism' and to discourage mental translation. Here's an example:

What's this?	It's a piece of chalk.
What's the colour of it?	It's white.
Who's holding it?	You are.
What am I doing with it?	You're writing with it.
What am I writing on?	You're writing on the blackboard.

Etc.

(1921a)

To ensure that learners are familiar with the vocabulary in these exchanges, unfamiliar items are either translated on the spot, or learners memorize word lists in advance of the lesson.

An important principle for Palmer was what he called 'gradation': 'Gradation means passing from the known to the unknown by easy stages, each of which serves as a preparation for the next [...] In the ideally graded course the student is caused to assimilate perfectly a relatively small but exceedingly important vocabulary; when perfectly assimilated, this nucleus will develop and grow in the manner of a snowball' (1921b). Palmer also came to recognize that the mental lexicon consists of more than individual words. Rather, fluency is a function of having a store of memorized 'word-groups' – what we might now call 'lexical chunks'. As he wrote in 1925 (translated in Smith 1999): 'Progress in conversation is proportionate to the number of common and useful word-groups perfectly memorised by the student'. Later, Palmer was to extend this insight to encompass 'sentence patterns', prefiguring the pattern drills of **audiolingualism** (see chapter **6**).

Finally, and all being well, the more advanced student might be allowed to take part in what Palmer called 'normal conversation' – where the students talks and the teacher gently prompts with 'a quiet and leisurely suggestion from time to time' (1921a) while resisting the urge to correct every error as it occurs.

Does it work?

There are so many features of the Oral Method that have subsequently been validated by research into SLA that is hard not to think that, in the right hands, it must have been effective. Among these features are: the value of implicit learning; the importance of 'comprehensible input'; the need to associate form and meaning; the role of automaticity; the part that formulaic language plays in fluency, and the usefulness of 'scaffolding' the learner's output. The single most negative aspect of the approach is, perhaps, Palmer's obsession with accuracy: 'The principle of accuracy requires that *the student shall have no opportunities for making mistakes until he has arrived at this stage in which accurate work is reasonably to be expected*' (1921b). It is now generally agreed that errors are not only an inevitable part of language learning, but that, with appropriate feedback, they provide powerful learning opportunities.

What's in it for us?

Harold Palmer has been rightly credited with establishing ELT as a profession in its own right, and (along with his contemporaries Daniel Jones and A.S. Hornby) for laying the foundations of what came to be known as applied linguistics. He combined an intuitive feel for sound pedagogy with a scholarly, often innovative, understanding of how language works. For these reasons alone, he is worth re-visiting. But what particularly resonates is his intuition that proficiency is, first and foremost, the result of having a store of memorized phrases or expressions (see chapter **11 The Lexical Approach**).

Palmer, H. (1921a) *The Oral Method of Teaching Languages*. Cambridge: Heffer.

Palmer, H. (1921b) *The Principles of Language Study*. London: Harrap.

Smith, R. (1999) *The Writings of Harold E. Palmer: An Overview*. Tokyo: Hon-no-Tomosha.

5 The Reading Method

> The major impact of the Reform Movement was to shift the emphasis away from literacy and on to the teaching of the spoken language. The Reading Method was unusual in attempting to reverse this trend.

The background

What's the easiest, least stressful way of getting a foothold into a foreign language – especially if time is at a premium? Arguably, it might be through reading, especially reading of texts that are not only intrinsically interesting, but are graded to the learner's level of competence.

This, at least, was the conclusion reached by Algernon Coleman, whose report on the state of foreign language teaching in the US, published in 1929, challenged the current view that oral and written fluency were desirable and achievable instructional outcomes. Coleman noted that most students in American schools studied a foreign language for at most two years: not nearly enough time to be able to speak the language at anything beyond the most basic level of proficiency. He proposed, therefore, that a more realistic objective might be (as he put it) 'the ability to read the foreign language with moderate ease and with enjoyment for recreative and for vocational purposes' (1929/1930).

The 'Coleman report' had considerable influence, offering an antidote to the culture of failure: through reading, learners could achieve a 'critical mass' of familiarity with the target language which might, in turn, serve as a springboard for subsequent development of the skills of speaking and writing, should the learners need them. Having been widely adopted for the teaching of foreign languages in the US, the Reading Method spread to other contexts, such as India, and was adapted for the teaching of English, principally by Michael West, whose 'New Method Readers' were based on the word frequency counts that

West would later publish as *The General Service List of English Words* (1953), the forerunner of modern corpus-based frequency lists.

How does it work?

In an article published in 1937, West provides us with a description of the basic stages of a typical lesson:

- The teacher introduces the new words of the section [of the text]; gives the meaning of each and gives some drill so as to fix it in the mind.
- The teacher makes sure that the pupils understand the questions [that accompany the text].
- The pupils read the questions; then they read the book and search for the answers. (This reading is done in a low whisper. Silent reading is not used until pupils can read faster than they speak.)
- When everyone has finished reading, the pupils write the answers.
- The teacher checks to see that the answers are right.
- Some reading aloud may follow.

The texts used in the Reading Method take the form of graded readers, i.e. simplified texts, graded according to measures of word frequency, the easiest texts being those using only the most frequent words in the language. Words likely to be unfamiliar are pre-taught or defined in footnotes, but only in the target language: there is no use of translation, on the assumption (shared by the **Direct Method**, see chapter 3) that use of the students' own language would interfere with or inhibit fluid reading. Students are also encouraged to infer the meaning of unfamiliar words from the context. The learning of vocabulary from word lists, again organized according to frequency, is another key ingredient of the method. But there is little or no overt teaching of grammar, apart from some basic structures and inflections without which comprehension would be at risk. Writing tasks are also limited to those that provide practice of the vocabulary and grammar that have been previously studied.

Speaking is limited to answering questions about the texts and reading aloud: proponents of the Reading Method recognized that reading fluency was facilitated when learners could relate the written word to the spoken one. Hence, in the first lessons learners are introduced to the sound system of the target language. Reading aloud enables them to 'hear' the written word in their 'mind's ear', as preparation for later silent reading.

A distinction is made between intensive reading and extensive reading. The former is developed by close reading of individual sentences, short texts, or parts of a text, so as to extract every detail, including features of the grammar. Extensive reading involves the students working on their own, reading longer texts. For both reading modes, comprehension is typically checked by the teacher asking questions.

Does it work?

The Reading Method was a practical response to a real educational dilemma – and one that persists to this day – i.e. how do you balance the need for second language learning with the limited time available for it in mainstream education? By focusing on comprehension alone, the method offered the potential to 'fast-track' learners into a working familiarity with the language without the anxiety associated with the need to speak or write it. For West, the Reading Method was a precursor to speech: 'Learning to read a language before learning to speak it has the advantage that when the pupil begins to speak he possesses some general idea of the form of the language and some sense of right or wrong idiom' (1937).

In this sense, it anticipates by half a century the principle of 'comprehensible input' as argued by Stephen Krashen (see chapters **2 The Natural Method/Approach** and **7 Total Physical Response**). Moreover, the staged approach to reading, including familiarizing learners with the sound system, and the use of reading aloud as a means of consolidating the relationship between printed text and spoken word, offers a plausible – if neglected – pedagogy for the teaching of receptive skills generally. Also, the emphasis placed on acquiring a sizeable vocabulary conforms to the view that the more words you know, the easier it will be to read authentic texts. (It has not been conclusively shown, though, that the more you read, the more words you will learn: it seems that, unless attention is consciously directed at unfamiliar words, they tend to go 'in one eye and out the other'.) And the use of texts to embed features of grammar, and as a vehicle for teaching them, is consistent with the view that grammar is best learned in context.

Unsurprisingly perhaps, research into extensive reading seems to confirm the view that 'extensive reading improves students' reading proficiency' (Nakanishi 2014), although – as mentioned – the effects on other areas of language development, such as vocabulary growth, are less conclusive.

On the down side, an exclusive focus on developing reading skills might reasonably frustrate learners who equate proficiency in a second language with spoken fluency. Nowadays, it would be difficult to 'sell' the idea of a language school where the main focus was on reading. Also, if learners are not yet skilled readers in their first language, they may have difficulty developing these skills in a second.

What's in it for us?

There is a refreshing sense of pragmatism in the Reading Method which acts as a useful counterbalance to the almost obsessive focus on spoken fluency that distinguishes most language teaching methods of the last 100 years. For many learners, speaking a second language is a highly stressful experience. Reading, on the other hand, seldom is. Gently graduating from receptive skills to productive skills may alleviate some of the anxiety associated with second language learning.

Coleman, A. (1929/1930) *The Teaching of Modern Foreign Languages in the United States.* New York: Macmillan.

Nakanishi, T. (2015) A meta-analysis of extensive reading research. *TESOL Quarterly*, 49/1: 6–37.

West, M. (1937) The "Reading Approach" and "The New Method System". *Modern Language Journal*, 22/3: 220–222.

West, M. (1953) *A General Service List of English Words.* London: Longman.

6 The Audiolingual Method

The image of a class of language students wearing headsets and confined to the narrow cubicles of a language laboratory neatly captures the confluence of scientific method, technological innovation and structural linguistics that gave birth to audiolingualism. But was it as bad as it looked?

The background

'TO LEARN A NEW LANGUAGE ONE MUST ESTABLISH ORALLY THE PATTERNS OF THE LANGUAGE AS SUBCONSCIOUS HABITS' (Lado 1943/1970, emphasis in original).

In this fashion, the founding principle of the method that would be known as the audiolingual method was (loudly) proclaimed. Robert Lado (author of the above) was born in Florida of Spanish parents who moved back to Spain before Lado had had a chance to acquire English. On his return to the US, aged 21, he started learning English for the first time – thus giving him a privileged insight into second language learning, and also into the differences between Spanish and English. Out of this experience, Lado developed an interest in contrastive linguistics, which he studied at the University of Michigan's English Language Institute (ELI) under its director, the structural linguist Charles Fries.

At the time, a furious effort was being made to develop intensive language learning programs as part of the war effort. The **Reading Method** (see chapter 5) had resulted in a generation ill-equipped to converse fluently in other languages. Respected linguists, like Leonard Bloomfield, were recruited to advise on the problem. Fries and Lado took up the challenge, each bringing their unique expertise to the enterprise: Fries his interest in the structures – or patterns – of languages, and Lado his belief that it was the differences between languages that were the cause of learning difficulty.

Out of their collective efforts evolved the Audiolingual Method (so called because an earlier name, the Aural-oral Method, was difficult to pronounce!). Adapted to the emerging technologies of the time, it provided the methodology for programmed learning. It was widespread in the 1950s, particularly in the US, peaked in the mid-1960s, and then virtually disappeared without trace – only to return in recent years in the guise of adaptive learning apps (see chapter **28 Programmed Instruction: Duolingo**).

How does it work?

In his best known book, *The Structure of English* (1952), Fries argued, 'if adults of foreign speech are to learn English they must, among other things, learn to respond to and to give the signals by which a language conveys its structural meanings. The most efficient materials for such learning are those that are based upon an accurate descriptive analysis of the structural patterns'. Accordingly, lists of sentence patterns were devised, such as these (from the contents of the book that Lado helped produce in 1943):

Lesson IV

1. WHEN DID YOU ARRIVE? [Word order of questions with WHAT, WHEN, WHERE, WHO(M)]
2. I'M STUDYING GRAMMAR. WHAT ARE YOU STUDYING? [AM, IS, ARE + the -ING form of a Class 2 word in statements and questions]
3. IT'S A GOOD CLASS. IT'S A GRAMMAR CLASS. [Single word modifiers before Class 1 words]

The two basic principles on which the teaching of these patterns was based were habit formation (through repetition) and avoidance of translation (through fear of L1 interference). Both were core tenets of the **Direct Method** (see chapter **3**) that were simply adopted and refined, and both were justified on the grounds that they characterize first language acquisition (which is why we are labelling audiolingualism a *natural* approach). Because imitation – i.e. mimicry – and memorization were prototypical practices, the method was sometimes called the Mim-mem Method.

Only later were developments in behavioural psychology enlisted to support the case for habit formation. But, even before stimulus-response-reinforcement became the name of the game, the defining activity of the audiolingual method was the pattern practice drill. Here is how Lado (1943/1970) describes it:

> In PATTERN PRACTICE ... the student is led to practice a pattern, changing some element of that pattern each time, so that normally he never repeats the same sentence twice. Furthermore, his attention is drawn to the changes, which are stimulated by pictures, oral substitutions, etc., and thus the PATTERN ITSELF, THE SIGNIFICANT FRAMEWORK OF THE SENTENCE, rather than the particular sentence, is driven intensively into his habit reflexes.

Developments in technology, including the language laboratory, would make this mechanical practice more mechanical still, but would at least relieve the teacher of the need to become a drill-master. But it was not all drilling. Here's how a typical lesson might be structured, according to an audiolingual textbook of its time, called *English through Patterns* (Ramsey 1969):

> New patterns are introduced at the beginning of each lesson through a dialog or a serialised story ... *Structures* are presented in frames followed by: A) *Exercise*, which serves as an explanatory device, B) *Drill*, designed to establish the new structure as an automatic response, C) *Practice*, where the student is required to use the structure in a less restricted framework and thereby assure his comprehension and control.

Does it work?

At the theoretical level, the audiolingual method suffered many reverses. For a start, contrastive analysis (e.g. between Spanish and English) failed to predict many of the errors that learners typically make, suggesting that errors were not necessarily 'bad habits'. And then there was Noam Chomsky's celebrated attack on the fundamentals of behaviourism, which seemed to confirm what a number of methodologists had suspected all along: that imitation alone cannot account for linguistic creativity.

There was a certain injustice, though, in branding the Audiolingual Method as simply mindless parroting. In the introduction to the textbook quoted above, the author writes, 'At no time are students to parrot meaningless phrases. Learning, as far as we're concerned, is a thinking process. Variety makes for an interesting class. Intense drill should be interspersed with other activities such as: Chart Practice ..., controlled conversation, language games, quizzes, etc.' (Ramsey 1967). And, in an updated edition of the University of Michigan's *English Sentence Patterns*, the author insists, 'probably the best way to practice a foreign language is to use it in communicating with others. Thus, teachers should provide time for meaning-oriented practice' (Krohn 1971).

Nevertheless, the emphasis on accurate learning in incremental steps before 'meaningful-oriented practice' was allowed, as well as the strict rationing of vocabulary input, put a strong brake on the development of fluency.

What's in it for us?

Old school audiolingualists may be taking heart in developments in SLA theory that suggest that, yes, environmental factors (such as exposure to frequently occurring patterns) do impact on learning. So-called usage-based theories, drawing on the way that neural networks are strengthened by patterns in the input, sound remarkably like old-style behaviourism. What's more, they seem to vindicate repetitive practice in order to counteract entrenched L1 'habits'. Also, related developments in corpus linguistics have reinforced the view that language is both intricately patterned and remarkably formulaic. This suggests that the memorization of prototypical examples of patterns and also of commonly-occurring formulaic 'chunks' may benefit both fluency and the acquisition of grammar. Is it time to bring back the language laboratory?

Fries, C. (1952) *The Structure of English: An Introduction to the Construction of English Sentences*. New York: Harcourt Brace.

Krohn, R. (1971) *English Sentence Structure*. Ann Arbor: University of Michigan Press.

Lado, R. (1943/1970) 'Introduction' to Lado, R. and Fries, C. *English Pattern Practice: Establishing the Patterns as Habits*. Ann Arbor: University of Michigan Press.

Ramsey, R. (1967) *English Through Patterns*. Barcelona: Teide.

7 Total Physical Response

> The ease with which children acquire their first –
> and, often, a second – language has long fascinated
> methodologists. Could the fact that they physically
> *embody* the language have something to do with it?

The background

In the late nineteenth century, a Frenchman called François Gouin,
having failed to learn German by traditional methods (including
memorizing a dictionary), had a flash of insight on observing his young
nephew recounting a visit to the local mill. The boy's story took the
form of the description of a sequence of activities, inspiring Gouin
to develop his 'series method': lessons consisted of series of actions
that were simultaneously enacted and described. In addition, Gouin's
observations of children's language learning suggested to him the need
for an 'incubation period' between listening and speaking. Not only was
Gouin's approach a precursor of the **Direct Method** (see chapter 3) but
his recognition of the need for a 'silent period' also presaged the **Natural
Approach** of Terrell and Krashen (see chapter 2).

Gouin's influence was considerable, especially in the teaching of foreign
languages in schools, and it persisted into the twentieth century.
For Gouin, the key to language was the verb, and the structure that
highlights verbs like nothing else is the imperative. Harold Palmer
(of the **Oral Method**, see chapter 4) developed this idea into what he
called 'imperative drill': 'The teacher says "get up", and makes the
appropriate sign. The student has not understood the words but he does
understand the sign and he gets up. The teacher says "sit down" and the
student obeys the gesture' (Palmer 1921). Once students are trained to
associate the command with the action, the gestures are withheld. And
the commands increase in complexity – from 'get up' to 'take the fourth
book from the side nearest the window, from the second shelf; open it at
page 65 and point to the first word' (ibid.). For Palmer it was important
that students remain silent during the performance of the actions.

It took another four decades before this technique was developed into a method in its own right, to be called Total Physical Response (TPR). It's perhaps significant that one of the early papers published on it by the method's architect, James Asher, was called 'Children's first language as a model for second language learning' (Asher 1972). In that article, Asher argues that 'not only is listening critical for the development of speaking, but children acquire listening skill in a particular way. For instance, there is an intimate relationship between language and the child's body'. It is this intimate relationship that TPR seeks to exploit for second language learning.

How does it work?

Just as in Palmer's 'imperative drills', Asher's approach revolves around sets of instructions, using pre-taught vocabulary referring to real objects that can be brought into the classroom. The teacher demonstrates the actions and individual students join her to perform them. Once the students are sufficiently 'well trained', the teacher repeats the instructions without enacting them and the students, either individually or as a group, perform them. The commands are varied using new combinations of the basic ingredients. At no point are students encouraged to repeat them.

A typical sequence might go like this:

> Igor, pick up the black box. Give it to Juana.
> Juana, put the red car in the box. Walk to the door with the box. Leave the box by the door.
> Keiko, point at the black box. Go to the box. Take out the red car. Hand it to Johan. Ana, walk to the board. Draw a fish. Write 'fish'.

> Etc.

After a number of lessons like this, students are given lists of the basic instructions they have been exposed to, and asked to study these as homework. They are then given the chance to speak, by first preparing their own commands using new combinations of the linguistic elements (*pick up, give, point to, draw; box, car, fish*, etc.), and then instructing their classmates to perform them.

Obviously, there are severe limitations in terms of the structural complexity of the input if it is limited solely to commands. Asher himself had ingenious suggestions for incorporating a greater range of structures into the method. Subsequently, Blaine Ray, a high school teacher of Spanish in California, experimented with ways of including narrative-building activities with a view to extending the linguistic range of the input. He trademarked the approach that resulted as TPRS (standing for Teaching Proficiency through Reading and Storytelling). The basic technique involves the teacher eliciting from the learners a story (typically fantastic) that involves a good deal of recycling of structures and vocabulary. The story is both acted out and re-told by the learners, and serves as the basis for further listening and reading activities. Comprehension at all stages is closely monitored, using techniques such as eliciting occasional L1 translations, or 'teaching to the eyes', i.e. closely observing learners' degree of understanding through eye contact and body language.

Does it work?

Initial research into TPR (admittedly, by Asher himself) indicated positive gains, compared to classes taught by audiolingual methods, not only in listening skills (as you would expect) but in other skills, including speaking, suggesting that there had been some kind of internalization of the grammar – although grammar had never been explicitly taught or drilled. Similar claims have been made for the efficacy of TPRS. However, as in all comparison studies of methods, considerable caution has to be exercised, given the difficulty of controlling for all the variables. Moreover, few, if any, of these studies were conducted over the long term, so it's difficult to know how these gains might be sustained. Finally, comparing TPR (or TPRS) with audiolingualism seems hardly relevant nowadays, given the almost total demise of the latter.

What's in it for us?

TPR is now generally considered as a set of techniques that can be integrated into other methods, principally the Natural Approach. However, the notion of a 'silent period', during which learners are exposed to comprehensible input before they are required to speak, is an attractive one, if for no other reason that it takes some of the anxiety out of initial learning. More compelling, perhaps, is the holistic and 'embodied' nature of learning in TPR. The idea that learning involves more than purely mental operations or – put another way – that cognition extends beyond the physical brain, is gaining hold nowadays. Research into first language learning has shown that acting out word meanings facilitates their learning; research in SLA – in, for example, the learning of phrasal verbs – is showing similar benefits. Asher argued that bodily movement, including gesture, is 'a powerful mediator' for the storage of linguistic input (1983). It seems that it might also be a powerful mediator for the retrieval and control of output. Encouraging the use of gesture and movement in the language classroom, by both teachers and learners, upholds a tradition begun by Gouin and further refined in the work of Palmer and Asher.

Asher, J. (1972) Children's first language as a model for second language learning. *Modern Language Journal*, 56: 133–139.

Palmer, H. (1921) *The Oral Method of Teaching Languages*. Cambridge: Heffer.

B: Linguistic methods

The next six methods are loosely labelled 'linguistic methods', since they are driven less by theories of learning than by theories of language. Language is seen as a property of the mind, and as such is best learned by engaging mental faculties, such as reason, attention, memory, and by the application of rules. Such methods make no pretence that the learning of a second language is 'natural'; on the contrary, it is an intellectual exercise with a strong focus on the formal features of the language – especially its grammar. Such a focus, though, does not necessarily ignore a concern for its communicative functions.

'With a fresh blotting-case under his arm, he set forth to attend the opening lecture of the course. Three hundred young men, bare-headed, filled an amphitheatre, where an old man in a red gown was delivering a discourse in a monotonous voice. Quill pens went scratching over the paper...' (*Sentimental Education*). In this fashion, Gustave Flaubert captures the essence of French education in the 19th century, of which *explication de texte* was a core technique.

The background

Explication de texte is French for 'text explication', but might better be translated as 'text analysis'. In fact *analyse de texte* is another French term for it, as is *lecture expliquée* (explicated, or explained, reading). All these terms attest to the strong associations that *explication de texte* has with the teaching of French: like dictation, *explication de texte* is embedded in French pedagogical practice, in teaching French both as a mother tongue, especially its literature, and as a foreign language – and it has a long history.

In fact, *explication de texte* goes back at least 2,000 years – to the classical tradition of *praelectio* (literally 'reading aloud') – where pupils in Ancient Rome were required to parse the grammar, scan the meter, and comment on the style of each line of the classical poem or play that they happened to be studying. The tradition persisted into the Renaissance and beyond, and was known as 'construing'. It merged with a tradition of Biblical scholarship (or *exegesis*).

It was not until the end of the eighteenth century, though, that *explication de texte* began to be applied to living languages. Combined with translation, it morphed into what became known as **Grammar-Translation** (see chapter 10). As a vehicle for the study and appreciation of literature, as well as for the teaching of first language literacy, it found a natural fit with the philological tradition of the French enlightenment, with its taste for formal stylistic analysis. For the teaching of foreign languages, and as a reaction to such Western practices as the direct method, in Soviet Russia it was re-branded as the 'conscious-comparative method', and, as such, was then exported to China.

How does it work?

An example from a textbook of the time shows how *explication de texte* was adapted to the teaching of English in the nineteenth century. The first book of T. Robertson's *New Course* (1851/1872) is ingeniously based on one single text, a folk tale translated into ungraded English. Each sentence of the story supplies the content of each of the course's 20 units. For example, the first sentence, and hence the first text that the learner meets, goes like this:

> We are told that the Sultan Mahmoud, by his perpetual wars abroad, and his tyranny at home, had filled the dominions of his forefathers with ruin and desolation, and had unpeopled the Persian empire.

Then follow twenty closely written pages in Spanish (because this is the version of the course designed for Spanish speakers), providing a key to the pronunciation, a translation, exercises for translation, and then a section titled 'Analysis, Theory and Synthesis' (women and children are advised to skip this section) in which every word is subject to detailed 'explication' for what it reveals about English phonology, morphology or syntax. *Unpeopled*, for example, exemplifies the way that the prefix *un-* negates the meaning of some verbs, while the suffix *–ed* forms the past participle. The same procedure is adopted for each of the subsequent 19 segments of the text.

The teacher's notes for the course recommend that the text be written on the board and that the book be kept closed during the lesson. The teacher orchestrates a succession of tasks, including reading aloud, translation, question and answer, dictation, and the re-combining of elements of the text to create new phrases or sentences. By the end of the lesson, students are expected to have learned the text by heart.

A variation of this method was (accidentally) invented by a teacher of French in the late 18ᵗʰ century. Jean Joseph Jacotot (1770–1840) was unexpectedly required to teach French to speakers of Flemish, a language he knew nothing of. Unable to use translation, he nevertheless had his students get copies of a French novel. Using the book as a kind of corpus, the students were set the task of reading the text, a word at a time, and searching the text for further examples of the same words or structures. Gradually, they were able not only to make sense of the book but also to acquire the basics of the grammar. From this experience, Jacotot concluded that learners were able to teach themselves with little overt guidance, and that a single book could embody a microcosm of the language as a whole.

Does it work?

The reliance on explanation, with its associated terminology, and on translation, places *explication de texte* firmly in the non-natural method camp. Like Grammar-Translation (to which it is akin), such an approach may suit certain kinds of learners more than others, e.g. those with a scholarly learning style and with less need to put the language to communicative use. Those in a hurry, however, may find the approach frustrating.

Of course, it's not impossible to imagine a 'lighter' version of *explication de texte*, where, for a start, the texts are graded, and where the individual sentences demonstrate features of grammar and vocabulary which have been selected as appropriate to the learners' developmental stage.

Nevertheless, research suggests that there is little or no correlation between metalinguistic knowledge (knowledge *about* the language) and communicative ability. That is to say, knowing that *un-* is a negative prefix does not automatically transfer into the capacity to make negative statements. Moreover, the risk of the teacher taking over, and lecturing at length about grammar and style, at the expense of any learner involvement or engagement, makes the wholesale adoption of the approach risky, to say the least. This is where an adapted version of *explication de texte* – in the style of Jacotot – which is less teacher- or book-centred, and which involves the learners collaborating to solve language puzzles in a text – might be a viable option.

What's in it for us?

Communicative Language Teaching – for many, the current orthodoxy – has often been criticised for the somewhat superficial approach it takes to dealing with texts. Skimming and scanning a written text, or extracting the gist from a spoken text, are encouraged. But 'close' reading or listening are less often dealt with in many current materials. Arguably, this is a loss: texts are under-exploited for what they might reveal about a whole range of linguistic features – lexical, grammatical and textual. *Explication de texte* – preferably learner-led and collaborative – offers a methodology for this kind of more penetrating analysis. And, without needing to venture too far into exegesis or literary criticism, 'critical reading' encourages learners (typically at more advanced levels) to critically engage with, and 'interrogate' texts, in order to uncover their ideological subtexts.

Robertson, T. (1851/1872) *Nuevo curso de idioma inglés escrito por los franceses (8th edition)*. New York: Appleton & Co.

'The study of a language is in its essence a series of acts of memorizing,' wrote Harold Palmer in 1921. 'Whether we are concerned with isolated words, with word-groups, with meanings or with the phenomena of grammar, the fact remains that successful memorizing is the basis of all progress.' It stands to reason, then, that a method that foregrounds memorization has a lot going for it.

The background

Memorization – also known as *rote-learning* and *learning by heart* – is institutionalized in a number of educational traditions. Combined with recitation, it is – or has been – standard practice in religious schools in many parts of the world. Knowing a sacred text by heart is believed to be a prerequisite for understanding and interpreting it. Once the text has been internalized in this way, it is available for study and commentary and, especially in the days before print, for further dissemination.

The tradition has permeated secular education in many cultures. Confucian-heritage educational systems, for example, are often (perhaps undeservedly) equated with a culture of imitation and rote-learning. The education system in South Korea is frequently cited as an extreme example of this heritage, with children cramming for high-stakes exams from an early age. The sight of students memorizing long lists of English words on their way to and from school is a common one.

Memorization is not confined to Asia, of course. Until relatively recently, it was well-established in education systems in the west, either directly (e.g. through choral chanting and drilling) or indirectly (as a consequence of the exam system). Only a few years ago, the then Minister of Education in the UK was reported as saying, 'memorisation is a necessary precondition of understanding'. In this fashion, the case for rote-learning – as opposed to other, more experiential forms of learning – is regularly championed, and continues to divide opinion: it clearly has a strongly ideological basis.

In English language teaching, support for memorization as a technique – if not a method in its own right – has fluctuated. It is now most often associated with the **Audiolingual Method** (which at one time was called the *Mim-mem Method*, standing for mimicry and memorization, see chapter 6). Repetitive drilling is the technique by means of which sentence patterns were supposedly entrenched in memory as habits. Dialogues which embedded these sentence patterns were learned by heart. When the behaviourist learning theory underpinning audiolingualism was discredited, memorization fell out of favour too. 'Mindless parroting' is what its detractors called it.

Much earlier, memorisation of sentences and whole texts was a feature of a number of 19th century approaches. Thomas Prendergast (see chapter **26 Prendergast's 'Mastery System'**) developed an original version of Grammar-Translation which involved translating grammatically complex sentences with a view to memorizing them, manipulating them, and internalizing their grammatical elements. He maintained that 'the power of speaking other tongues idiomatically is attained principally by efforts of the memory, not by logical reasonings' (1864).

Earlier still, Jean Joseph Jacotot (1770–1840) had made his learners memorize complete novels (see chapter **8** *Explication de Texte*) which would then become a linguistic resource into which they could search and retrieve – in much the same way as we might now search an online corpus. As Howatt and Smith (2000) observe, 'the texts themselves are largely irrelevant: they are not like prayers to be repeated verbatim but are important for what they can yield if they are taken to pieces and used in appropriate circumstances'.

The idea of using memorized texts as a resource persists to this day in, among other places, China. As in the memorizing of sacred texts, it is felt that only when a text has been appropriated in this way is it optimally available as an object for study and a tool for learning.

How does it work?

In a study of three exceptional learners of English in China (Ding 2007), all attested to the usefulness of text memorization. The way that this was implemented in one class involved the following stages:

- having worked on a written text in their coursebook in class, students then listen to a recording of it;
- they attempt to imitate the spoken text, intonation included, sometimes listening to the text up to 50 times;
- they continue to practise at home, and, in subsequent lessons, are individually tested on their ability to recall the text;
- they are set regular tests involving recall of phrases and sentence patterns based on the memorized texts;
- eventually the students will have memorized all the texts in the coursebook.

According to Ding, at more advanced levels, learners would commit to memory the entire screenplays of feature films, imitating the accent and prosody of each speaker.

Does it work?

All three students in the aforementioned study attribute their success in national English-speaking competitions to the practice of text memorization during their middle school years. They claim that it has given them a 'feel' for the language. More specifically, they seem to have each imported an enormous 'database' of English from which they can draw. As one of them reported, 'through reciting those lessons, he gained mastery of many collocations, phrases, sentence patterns and other language points' (Ding 2007).

On the other hand, in another study of Chinese learners (Gan et al. 2004), in which the learning strategies of successful and unsuccessful learners were compared, the researchers found that reliance on rote-learning alone was insufficient. While the unsuccessful students relied on memorizing word lists, successful students reinforced the learning of words by regular reading and attempting to put the memorized words to use. Also, the successful learners set learning goals and identified ways of achieving these, whereas the unsuccessful ones did not. While this study focused on the memorization of word lists rather than of whole texts, it does suggest that supplementing rote-learning with deliberate attempts to retrieve and use the memorized material is crucial.

What's in it for us?

It's unlikely that learners in cultures where the tradition does not already exist will take kindly to the suggestion that they should embark on text memorization on a scale as demanding as practised in China. Even in China, there is some resistance to the idea, and one of the learners in the Ding study admitted to disliking it at first. Nevertheless, many learners in a wide range of contexts pick up the words of English language songs, or the language uttered in video games, or catchphrases from TV shows, whether intentionally or not. Often, these memorized segments will emerge unexpectedly, but appropriately and accurately. Handled more systematically, the memorization of short texts, including dialogues, may offer a foothold into the language, and provide the 'feel' that other, more grammar-focused approaches, do not.

Ding, Y. (2007) Text memorization and imitation: The practices of successful Chinese learners of English. *System*. 35: 271–280.

Gan, Z., Humphreys, G., & Hamps-Lyon, L. (2004) Understanding successful and unsuccessful EFL students in Chinese universities. *Modern Language Journal*, 88: 229–244.

Howatt, A.P.R., & Smith, R.C. (2000) 'General introduction' to Howatt and Smith (eds.) *Foundations of Foreign Language Teaching: 19th Century Innovators*. London: Routledge.

Palmer, H. (1921) *The Oral Method of Teaching Languages*. Vonkers on Hudson, New York: World Book Company.

Grammar-Translation 10

In most teacher preparation courses in which the 'history of methods' is reviewed, it all began with Grammar-Translation. And it was bad! In fact, neither claim – that Grammar-Translation was the first method, and that it was inherently wrong – is entirely true.

The background

When I was a student of French at secondary school in New Zealand in the 1960s, the curriculum was based on a textbook called *A New French Course* (Horan & Wheeler 1963). The story-line followed the (fairly uneventful) life of the Ravel family, dramatized as short dialogues, but the syllabus was organized around a graded list of grammatical structures, one or two per unit. The English equivalents of these structures were provided, along with a list of thematically-related words. Exercises involving translating sentences from French into English, and then the reverse, provided the bulk of the practice.

All this will be familiar to many language learners, especially those who have studied modern languages at school. This is hardly surprising, perhaps, since the approach was originally devised to meet the needs of school children in the early nineteenth century, an age-group for whom the self-study, text-based methods of classics scholars were simply not appropriate. At one time called 'the Prussian Method', because it was developed and refined in what is now Germany, the twin focus on grammar and translation was a legacy of the study of classical (i.e. dead) languages. It was part of a long tradition that included the detailed analysis – or 'construing' – of literary texts (see chapter 8). But the preference for individual sentences, rather than whole texts, was an innovation. It was felt that the grammar focus could be more easily controlled and delimited this way. That the sentences were invented, and often bizarre, was unfortunate – and would eventually serve to discredit the method (dubbed Grammar-Translation by its detractors).

Here, for examples, are sentences for translation from Ollendorf's *Nuevo Método* (1876):

> What mattress have you? – I have the sailor's. – Have you his good beer or his fine meat? – I have neither this nor that. – Have you the corn of the Frenchman or that of the Englishman? – I have neither the Frenchman's nor the Englishman's, but that of my granary. Etc.

Since Grammar-Translation had originally been designed for schoolchildren, it adapted relatively well to the needs of a growing cosmopolitan middle class who needed foreign languages for trading goods and ideas, but were not versed in the classics. The grammar component of Grammar-Translation was kept relatively simple, with minimal use of terminology. However, over time, the temptation to include more and more grammatical padding, in the form of detailed explanations and long lists of exceptions to rules, became irresistible. This was in large part motivated by the reverence in which grammar was held: one course, published in Spain in 1825, posted the following quotation (by a certain John Horne Tooke) on its title page:

> I consider Grammar as absolutely necessary in the search for philosophical truth, and I think it no less necessary in the most important questions concerning religion and civil society.

The nineteenth century witnessed an unprecedented growth in the production of grammars of English, with grammarians vying with one another to slice the grammar cake into ever smaller portions, and this pedantry was reflected in its teaching texts. It was further compounded by the fact that the default model for grammatical description was still Greek and Latin, and the very different grammar of English was forced to comply with these classical models. Nevertheless, for the teaching of highly inflected languages like French or German, the rule-based approach seemed to make more sense – even if, as Kelly (1969) notes, 'language skill was equated with the ability to conjugate and decline'.

How does it work?

My French course was more or less typical: the obligatory elements of the Grammar-Translation lesson include a statement of the rule in the learner's L1; a translated list of vocabulary items, chosen so as to make a good fit with the grammar point; followed by translation exercises in and out of the target language. Eventually, the student might translate whole texts – especially for assessment purposes. Optional elements might include dialogues or texts that contextualize the syllabus items, as well as prompts for a 'conversation' using the same items. But the focus is very much on the written language, on accuracy and on the memorization of rules.

How teachers actually negotiate this material is very much up to them, since there is seldom any guidance provided as to how a Grammar-Translation lesson is realized in practice. In that sense, Grammar-Translation is a method without a methodology. The default approach is to work with the class in 'lockstep' (i.e. as one group), with individual learners taking turns to read lines of text aloud, and to translate sentences when called upon.

Does it work?

Given that Grammar-Translation was originally conceived as a means of cultivating literacy skills in the target language, including the ability to appreciate its literature, it would be unfair, perhaps, to judge it on its capacity to develop spoken fluency. Certainly, in the case of my French, it didn't. The almost exclusive focus on written forms, on sentence-level grammar, and on accuracy, means that – unless teachers incorporate free speaking activities into the lessons – there is zero preparation for spoken fluency. However, it's not hard to envisage a rehabilitated version of grammar-translation, where these weaknesses are counterbalanced, or even eliminated altogether – where the syllabus is more comprehensive, mediated by a balance of written and spoken texts, and with tasks that develop communicative competence.

One of Grammar-Translation's merits, however, is that, as Guy Cook (2010) points out, 'it may be particularly well suited to those teachers who are themselves not wholly proficient in the language they are teaching and/or too overworked to undertake extensive preparation'. In a sense, Grammar-Translation teaches itself, and this may be one of the main reasons for its enduring appeal.

What's in it for us?

It's ironic that, of the two defining features of Grammar-Translation, the grammar syllabus has survived, indeed flourished, while translation has been consistently – often vehemently – discouraged (even if it has been practised covertly). Yet translation has perhaps been unjustly denigrated: the direct method mantra that, in order to speak an L2 you have to think in it (with the corollary that, in order to think in it, you have to be submerged in it) has become an unshakeable dogma. But perhaps the real strength of Grammar-Translation was its (admittedly, somewhat pedestrian) use of translation, as a means of conveying meaning and of testing understanding, and as a way of entrenching the L2 grammar and vocabulary. Recent evidence from the field of neurobiology, including the use of neuroimaging techniques, seems to show that the languages of bilinguals are not differently located in the brain; rather, they share a common space. This fact alone might support a re-evaluation of the role of translation in the process of becoming bilingual.

Cook, G. (2010) *Translation in Language Teaching*. Oxford: Oxford University Press.

Horan, R.S., & Wheeler, J.R. (1963) *A New French Course*. Sydney: Science Press.

Kelly, L.G. (1969) *25 Centuries of Language Teaching*. Rowley, Mass: Newbury House.

Ollendorf, H.G. (1876) *Nuevo método para aprender a leer, escribir y hablar una lengua en seis meses. Aplicado al inglés (nueva edición)*. Paris: Ollendorf.

The Lexical Approach   11

In a radio broadcast in 1929, the English writer, Virginia
Woolf, had this to say: 'Words do not live in dictionaries:
they live in the mind. ... And how do they live in the
mind? Variously and strangely, much as human beings
live, ranging hither and thither, falling in love, meeting
together'. The way that words 'live in the mind', and what
this might mean for language teaching, is a major concern
of those who advocate a lexical approach.

The background

When asked *How does one achieve proficiency in a second language?*
Harold Palmer (see chapter **4 The Oral Method**) was unequivocal:
'*Memorize perfectly the largest number of common and useful word-
group*' (1925, quoted in Smith 1999). But it took the advent of
corpus linguistics to persuade researchers, such as John Sinclair, that
'learners would do well to learn the common words of the language
very thoroughly, because they carry the main patterns of the language'
(1991). And it wasn't until 1996 that COBUILD, under Sinclair's
supervision, produced a corpus-based pattern grammar of its own
(Francis et al. 1996), based on Sinclair's conviction that there is a close
relationship between word meanings and the patterns that they occur
with. Or, as Sinclair's eminent predecessor, J.R. Firth (1957), put it, 'you
shall know a word by the company it keeps'.

But it was a teacher, writer and publisher who was the first to attempt
to take this mixed bag of constructs – word groups, collocations,
patterns, formulaic language, syntactical constructions and so on – and
to base a teaching approach upon it. In 1993, Michael Lewis published
The Lexical Approach. It built on the success of his earlier book, *The
English Verb* (1986), and reflected an ongoing interest in pedagogical
grammar – with the significant difference being Lewis's reappraisal of

the relative importance of sentence grammar, on the one hand, and lexis (including multi-word 'chunks'), on the other. Whereas structuralist approaches had foregrounded grammatical patterns into which a restricted vocabulary was 'slotted', Lewis argued that language was primarily lexical, and that the 'kit of rules' that constitutes a grammar serves merely to link and fine-tune the meanings encoded in words. In short, as he famously claims in his list of 'key principles' at the start of his book: 'Language consists of grammaticalised lexis, not lexicalised grammar' (1993).

How does it work?

Although labelled an 'approach', Lewis's brainchild was somewhat short on the kind of detail that normally defines a method, such as how an entire course using the lexical approach might be sequenced or implemented. One pioneering attempt to incorporate the findings of corpus research into course design and base a syllabus entirely on frequency data was *The Collins COBUILD English Course* (Willis & Willis 1988), which was predicated on the view that 'the commonest and most important, most basic meanings in English are those meanings expressed by the most frequent words in English' (Willis 1990). Accordingly, the first book in the series was based on the 700 most frequent words in English, and the kinds of constructions that they typically occur in.

Lewis, however, is highly sceptical as to the value of additive, discrete-item syllabuses, whether of grammar items or of words ('I am concerned to establish a lexical approach, not a lexical syllabus'). He tends to align himself with Stephen Krashen's view that acquisition is best facilitated by exposure to comprehensible input, in the form of texts: 'A central requirement of the Lexical Approach is that language material should be text and discourse rather than sentence based' (op. cit.). He proposes a pedagogical cycle of *observing, hypothesizing* and *experimenting*, where selected and preferably authentic, texts are subjected to tasks that promote the noticing and manipulation of such lexical features as collocations and fixed and semi-fixed expressions, and where comparison between the target language and the students' L1 is encouraged.

Lindstromberg and Boers (2008) elaborate on this basic model, with a 'three-stage programme for chunk learning', which aims:

1 to help students notice chunks and appreciate their importance;
2 to deliberately target selected sets of chunks and apply techniques known to help students commit chunks to memory;
3 to consolidate knowledge through review.

Typical activities involve learners scanning texts for possible chunks and checking these against information in a dictionary or in an online corpus.

Does it work?

Because the lexical approach has seldom if ever been realized as a stand-alone method but, instead, has been integrated into existing methods, such as Communicative Language Teaching, or Text-based Instruction, it is difficult to assess its true effectiveness. Certainly, there has been a renewed interest in vocabulary teaching, including the teaching of collocation and other multi-word items, in recent years, and this is reflected in most current teaching materials. Moreover, research suggests that a critical mass of vocabulary is a prerequisite for both receptive and productive fluency, and that – as Palmer long ago argued – the more chunks, the greater the fluency. Retrieving chunks as opposed to individual words both saves processing time and confers a degree of idiomaticity (i.e. the capacity to sound natural) on the user. Hence, any approach that promotes the acquisition of formulaic language can only benefit the learner.

Unhappily, though, there are few if any innovative procedures that the lexical approach has offered us. Scanning texts for lexical chunks is like scanning the night sky for constellations: unless you already know what you are looking for, it is a fairly hit-and-miss business.

What's in it for us?

When Lewis first formulated his lexical approach it was grounded in a theory of *language* (i.e. that 'much language consists of multi-word "chunks"') but it lacked a coherent theory of *learning*. Since then, such a theory has emerged. A *usage-based* theory of language acquisition lends support to Lewis's basic premise. It argues that, through exposure to rich sources of real language use, certain frequently encountered sequences – called *constructions* – and their associated meanings are stored in memory and can be retrieved and re-combined for future use. Over time, using the innate human capacity to identify patterns, the internal structure (i.e. the grammar) of these constructions is unpacked, providing a model for the creation of novel utterances. The theory suggests that there is a strong case for viewing language less as independent systems of grammar and vocabulary, and more as a spectrum of meaningful units ranging from individual morphemes (*-ing, -ed*) to abstract syntactic structures (verbs with two objects) by way of collocations (*highly likely, safe and sound*) – with lexis occupying a central role. While not fully validating a lexical approach, a usage-based theory does seem to confirm the view that teaching that is based on the rigid separation of grammar and vocabulary misrepresents both the means and the ends of language learning.

Firth, J.R. (1957) *Papers in Linguistics*. London: Oxford University Press.

Francis, G., Hunston, S., & Manning, E. (1996) *Collins COBUILD Grammar Patterns 1: Verbs*. London: HarperCollins.

Lewis, M. (1993) *The Lexical Approach: The State of ELT and a Way Forward*. Hove: Language Teaching Publications.

Lindstromberg, S., & Boers, F. (2008) *Teaching Chunks of Language: From Noticing to Remembering*. Helbling.

Sinclair, J. (1991) *Corpus, Concordance, Collocation*. Oxford: Oxford University Press.

Smith, R. (1999) *The Writings of Harold E. Palmer: An Overview*. Tokyo: Hon-no-Tomosha.

Willis, D. (1990) *The Lexical Syllabus: A New Approach to Language Teaching*. London: Collins.

Willis, J., & Willis, D. (1988) *The Collins COBUILD English Course*. London: Collins.

Text-based Instruction   12

> 'Language always happens as text, and not as isolated words and sentences. From an aesthetic, social or educational perspective, it is the text which is the significant unit of language' (Kress 1985).

The background

This belief is held as fundamental by proponents of Text-based Instruction. It's a theory of language that strongly contrasts with the long-held view that the basic unit of language – at least from the point of view of syllabus design – is the sentence. Structural approaches to teaching – as in the **Audiolingual Method** (see chapter 6) – take the sentence, and the elements that compose it, as their starting point. The primacy of the sentence was given an added boost by Noam Chomsky (1957) who argued: 'From now on I will consider a *language* to be a set (finite or infinite) of sentences, each finite in length and constructed out of a finite set of elements'. Teaching a language, it followed, is teaching how its sentences are formed from these elements.

Functional approaches, however, have long recognized the fact that, when we look at language from the point of view of the *meanings* it expresses, the sentence is no longer pre-eminent. A communicative event, such as a shopping encounter, or a job interview, or an exchange of SMS messages, is constructed of much more than a succession of independent sentences. And some communications, such as a compliment ('Nice shirt!') or a road sign (*NO PARKING*) consist of single phrases. From a functional point of view, language is realized – not as sentences – but as *text*, whether spoken or written, and whether a single word or a 600-page novel.

An early study of how language in its contexts of use occurs as connected text was conducted in the markets of Tunisia: the researcher (Mitchell 1957) observed that buying and selling exchanges followed clearly defined stages, even if different configurations of context factors meant that there was considerable variation within these stages. The dynamic nature of the emerging conversation (the text), and the way it is shaped by its context, led Mitchell to conclude (1975):

> A text is a kind of snowball, and every word or collocation in it is part of its own context, in the wider sense of this term; moreover, the snowball rolls now this way, now that.

The same reciprocal relationship between text and context underpins Michael Halliday's theoretical model called *systemic functional linguistics* (SFL), the theory that, in turn, informs text-based instruction. Halliday takes the view that 'language is as it is because of what it has to do' (Halliday 1978). What it has to do is make meanings, and these meanings are realised as text. Put simply, 'text is the process of meaning; and a text is the product of that process' (Halliday 1981/2002). In other words, 'text' is both verb and noun – the process of making meanings in context, and the product of that process in the form of texts. Nowadays, we witness on a daily basis the way that this process-product dynamic is played out in the form of SMS messages, where the messages themselves are the traces of a communicative exchange. Learning to mean in a language is learning to 'text'.

How does it work?

The methodology of Text-based Instruction is essentially an Australian invention. It grew out of the teaching of literacy there, both first language literacy (to children) and second language literacy (to migrants). As well as aligning the curriculum to a syllabus of text-types (or *genres*), proponents of Text-based (also called Genre-based) Instruction advocate the explicit teaching of the formal features of each genre in close association with its social and cultural functions. In this sense, it is very much a non-natural method, and its practitioners are in fact hostile to the kind of experiential approach to literacy development known as 'process writing'. Knowing how to construct and interpret the kinds of texts that are privileged in a society is part of a child's (or migrant's) 'cultural capital' and should not be left to chance, they argue.

Accordingly, a typical teaching sequence (following Derewianka 1990) involves the *modelling* of a chosen genre, including situating it in its social-cultural context. The next stage is identifying its overall organization (or macrostructure) and the purposes and linguistic features (grammatical, lexical and textual) of each of its stages. This is followed by *joint construction*, where learners work together to recycle these generic features in the construction of a new text. The final stage is *individual construction*, involving cycles of drafting and revision, and eventual publication – or performance, since a similar sequence is adopted for teaching spoken genres, such as giving presentations, being interviewed for a job, and so on.

Does it work?

Because text-based teaching moves from the whole to the parts, rather than vice versa, it is notionally aligned to what is known as **Whole Language Learning** (see chapter **18**), a major tenet of which is that language is best learned in authentic, meaningful situations, and by engaging with whole texts – whether spoken or written. Any assessment of its effectiveness needs to show, as a minimum, that working in this direction is as viable as working from the parts to the whole, i.e. learning grammar and vocabulary and then combining these to construct texts. Even so, a syllabus that is firmly grounded in the learners' social and cultural needs, and which facilitates their integration into the target 'discourse community', is arguably better than one that is simply an arbitrary list of grammatical structures.

On the downside, the bias towards written rather than spoken language can make this approach somewhat dry and academic, and needs to be balanced with work on spoken genres. And, like any linguistic approach, there is the ever-present danger that lessons will become simply a 'chalk-and-talk' demonstration by the teacher – not helped by the load of linguistic terminology that this approach has inherited from systemic functional linguistics.

What's in it for us?

For learners whose discourse needs are predictable – e.g. those doing English for Specific Purposes (ESP) courses – a text-based approach makes a lot of sense, even if it forms just one thread in a more grammar-based syllabus. Moreover, the fact that a text-based approach has been used with success with young learners in their first language suggests that it may have a wider application than a purely academic one. At any age, learning to write texts that conform to certain generic features – such as reporting an excursion or a sports event – may be better preparation for second language literacy than simply 'free-expression'.

Chomsky, N. (1957) *Syntactic Structures*. The Hague: Mouton.

Derewianka, B. (1990) *Exploring How Texts Work*. Newtown NSW: Primary English Teaching Association.

Halliday, M.A.K. (1978) *Language as Social Semiotic: The Social Interpretation of Language and Meaning*. London: Arnold.

Halliday, M.A.K. (1981/2002) Text Semantics and Clause Grammar: How is a Text Like a Clause? Reprinted in Webster, J.J. (ed.) *On Grammar: Volume 1 Collected Works of M.A.K. Halliday*. London: Continuum.

Kress, G. (1985) *Linguistic Processes in Sociolinguistic Practice*. Geelong, Victoria: Deakin University Press.

Mitchell, T.F. (1957) The Language of Buying and Selling in Cyrenaica: A Situational Statement. Reproduced in Mitchell (1975) *Principles of Firthian Linguistics*. London: Longman.

The Comparative Method 13

Natural approaches attempt to recreate the conditions of first language acquisition, as if the mind were a blank slate on to which the new language can be inscribed. But the mind of the second language learner is not a blank slate. As one linguist puts it, 'Second language is looking into the windows cut out by the first language' (Ushakova 1994). The Comparative Method embraces this understanding.

The background

Why do many Spanish-speaking learners of English say 'I no eat fish'? Presumably, because in Spanish they would say 'No como pescado'. That, at least, was the assumption underlying the proliferation of contrastive analysis studies in the mid-20th century. It was an assumption, though, that fell into disrepute, after it was discovered that all learners, regardless of their L1, go through a phase of saying 'I no eat fish'. More recently, however, there has been a revival of interest in contrastive analysis, not least because the L1 has been shown to be as much a positive influence as a negative one. Indeed, researchers now talk less about 'interference' than they do about 'transfer'.

In the early days of contrastive analysis, those linguists working within the behaviourist tradition were interested in the structural differences between one language and another, predicting that these differences would cause problems for learners. As Robert Lado (1971) memorably expressed it:

> We assume that the student who comes in contact with a foreign language will find some features of it quite easy and others extremely difficult. Those elements that are similar to his native language will be simple for him, and those elements that are different will be difficult.

Contrastive analysis aimed to identify which elements were similar and which different, in order to plan teaching syllabuses that would accommodate the similarities, while focusing mainly on the differences. But the methodology associated with these syllabuses (i.e. the **Audiolingual Method:** see chapter 6) did not invite the learners themselves to participate in this analysis. It was felt that to do so would simply increase the risk of their being negatively influenced by their L1: better, therefore, to keep the L1 well away.

Elsewhere, however, the pedagogical applications of contrastive analysis had been quietly morphing into what would be called 'the Comparative Method' (or 'the dual-language method'). The impetus for this approach originated in what was known as 'the Prague School' – a group of linguists (not all of them Czech) working in the 1920s and 1930s, who shifted the prevailing focus on linguistic *structures* to a focus on the communicative *functions* of language, thereby paving the way for the kind of functional linguistics associated with Michael Halliday, and, by extension, **Communicative Language Teaching** (see chapter **15**).

Being linguists, they were interested in the similarities and differences between languages. But, unlike the American 'descriptivist' tradition, the more functionally-inclined Prague scholars were less concerned with the formal characteristics of the languages being compared than in the ways in which the forms actually function. That is to say, 'the elements of one language are compared in the light of the corresponding situation or function in the other language' (Fried 1968). Initially a tool for linguistic analysis, it was a short step to turn this technique into a method for teaching second languages.

How does it work?

Unlike **Grammar-Translation** (see chapter **10**), the Comparative Method does not place translation at the centre of its methodology. Rather, it uses texts that are already translated as a stimulus for raising awareness as to the similarities and differences between the learner's L1 and the target language. As Vilém Fried (1968), a leading Prague School associate, describes it: 'The student is systematically guided and made to realize the functional differences that exist between the foreign language … and his native tongue', and he adds: 'Two-way translation [i.e. translation from both the L1 into the L2, and vice versa] may not be excluded here'.

In more recent years, the use of the learners' home language as a cognitive scaffold for the development of the target language is known as a 'translanguaging pedagogy' (Garcia & Kleifgen 2010), and has been encouraged in multilingual classrooms. Activities include identifying cognates in the two languages (i.e. words like *taxi* that are the same or similar), writing bilingual 'identity texts' (i.e. autobiographical texts that mix the writer's different languages), and pairing learners from the same language background so that those who are more fluent can help those who are less so. While such practices are not necessarily typical of the Comparative Method as first conceived, they are certainly compatible with an approach that not only tolerates, but actively encourages, classroom bilingualism.

Does it work?

Despite a growing literature on the use of *code-switching* (i.e. switching from one language to another) in classrooms, the use of actual translation as a pedagogic tool in the teaching of English is under-researched. The few studies that have been done suggest that there are real learning benefits from what has been called 'contrastive metalinguistic input' (Scheffler 2012). Certainly, the evidence suggests that most students prefer learning situations where some kind of cross-linguistic comparison is an option. New knowledge, after all, is constructed on, and regulated by, prior knowledge: whether teachers approve of it or not, learners will always be translating 'in their heads'. It makes sense, then, to bring this internal process out into the open, so that it can be more effectively managed and shared. Moreover, the co-existence of more than one language in the classroom better reflects the reality of real language use in an increasingly multilingual world.

What's in it for us?

One obvious implication of adopting a comparative approach is that the teacher needs to be proficient in the learners' L1 (which, of course, will not always be feasible in situations where learners come from different first language backgrounds). It also assumes that there are materials available that support cross-linguistic comparison. As Fried pointed out all of 50 years ago, there is a real need 'to prepare foreign language teaching materials in consideration of the fact that the learner's mother tongue will always be present as a factor of interference or support in the teaching process' (1968). Of course, 'doing' comparative translation does not require published materials: there is no shortage of texts online in both their original and their translated versions that could usefully serve as material for cross-linguistic comparison. Equally exploitable are the kind of 'bad translations' that are delivered up by online translation software. Perhaps the biggest challenge, however, is to convince several generations of teachers and teacher educators raised according to Direct Method principles that the L1 is not an obstacle to learning the L2, but an asset.

Fried, V. (1968) Comparative linguistic analysis in language teaching. In Jalling, H. (ed.) *Modern Language Teaching*, London: Oxford University Press.

García, O., & Kleifgen, J. (2010) *Educating Emergent Bilinguals*. New York: Teachers' College Press.

Lado, R. (1971) *Linguistics Across Cultures: Applied Linguistics for Language Teachers*. Ann Arbor: University of Michigan Press.

Laufer, B., & Girsai, N. (2008). Form-focused instruction in second language vocabulary learning: a case for contrastive analysis and translation. *Applied Linguistics* 29: 694–716.

Scheffler, P. (2012) Theories pass. Learners and teachers remain. *Applied Linguistics*, 33, 5: 603–607.

Ushakova, T. N. (1994) Inner speech and second language acquisition: an experimental-theoretical approach. In Lantolf, J.P., & Appel, G. (eds), *Vygotskian Approaches to Second Language Research*, Hillsdale, NJ: Ablex.

C: Communicative methods

The next group of methods share a concern for the situated and social nature of language use. This is not to say that other methods do not recognize language's social function. But there was a growing tendency in the 20th century to move away from language descriptions that took a primarily formal (or structuralist) view of language to a view of language that foregrounded its communicative purposes. This shift in perspective required an associated shift in methodology, which culminated in what is known as the Communicative Approach.

14 The Situational Approach

'The material of the language lesson,' wrote Lionel Billows in 1961, 'is not language, but life itself; the language is the instrument we use to deal with the material, slices of experience'. One form that these 'slices of experience' take is the situation, and the Situational Approach was originally conceived as a way of making the situation 'the material of the language lesson'.

The background

In 1914, the Polish anthropologist Bronislaw Malinowski (1881–1942) travelled to Papua and thence to the adjacent Trobriand Islands, where he conducted a lengthy ethnographic study of the islanders. Out of the experience of transcribing their day-to-day talk, he concluded that language use is entirely context-dependent: 'Utterance and situation are bound up inextricably with each other and the context of situation is indispensable for the understanding of words' (1923).

Malinowski's insight was picked up by a number of (primarily British) linguists. As one of them worded it, 'to be a member of a speech community is to know what language behaviour fits what situation' (Mackey 1978). It was left to others, such as Michael Halliday, to attempt to identify the ways that situational (or contextual) features are encoded (i.e. expressed) in language – a project that culminated in his *Introduction to Functional Grammar* (1985).

Meanwhile, the pedagogical implications of this 'situated' view of language were not lost on applied linguists. Pit Corder (1966) wrote that 'one can perfectly well envisage theoretically a course which had as its starting point an inventory of situations in which the learner would have to learn to behave verbally'.

While linguists were wrestling with these questions, teachers were already implementing what came to be known as Situational Language

Teaching. Lionel Billows' *Techniques of Language Teaching* (1961) outlines the principles that underpin this approach. In order to 'situate' language learning, Billows proposes a system of concentric circles, radiating out from the learner's immediate context (e.g. the classroom) to the world as directly experienced, the world as imagined, and the world as indirectly experienced through texts. Billows argues that we should always seek to engage the outer circles by way of the inner ones.

Teaching based around a syllabus of situations is best remembered in the form of the Audio-visual Method, popular in the teaching of French. However, it soon became apparent that 'situation' was too loose a way of categorising language in use, and, at best, was only good for generating a kind of 'phrase book' approach to syllabus design. So, apart from in some 'survival' courses for beginners, and in ESP courses (such as English for business people), the situation was largely abandoned as an organizing principle. Instead, it was co-opted into grammar-based courses in the **Oral Method** tradition (see chapter **4**), in the form of what Louis Alexander called 'structurally controlled situational teaching', i.e. 'teaching a language by means of a series of everyday situations while at the same time grading the structures which are presented' (1967). His *New Concept English* series (Alexander 1967) was a widely marketed example of this approach. *English in Situations* by Robert O'Neill (1970) further consolidated the basic model, in which the situation is simply a context for presenting the grammar.

How does it work?

The basic learning principle at work is that of induction, i.e. from the examples of a grammatical structure in a text or dialogue (typically presented orally), the learners work out the rules of its form and use. Here, for example, is a typical situation (from *English in Situations*, O'Neill 1970):

> Charles Gripp was a bank robber once. The police caught him in 1968 and he is in prison now. Before 1968 Charles drove a large car, robbed banks, had a lot of money and had arguments with his wife all the time. He did a lot of things then but he does not do any of those things now and he never sees his wife. HE USED TO BE A BANK

ROBBER. HE USED TO ROB BANKS, DRIVE A BIG CAR, AND
HAVE ARGUMENTS WITH HIS WIFE ALL THE TIME, BUT HE
DOESN'T DO ANY OF THOSE THINGS NOW.

The pattern may then be displayed in the form of a substitution table, and is consolidated through successive stages of controlled practice, beginning with imitation drills.

In somewhat elliptical style, O'Neill (1970) outlines the rationale:

> Class must have chance to gain insight into when to use pattern. Situations represent typical instances. From these, they can generalise about use of pattern. Teacher may also decide to give formal rule. However, this is not enough in itself. […] Formal rules can be helpful but cannot be substituted for student's own insight.

Does it work?

The 'generative situation' – i.e. a situation which generates several instances of the target structure – has provided legions of language teachers with an alternative to translation or explanation as a means of presenting grammar. As the first 'move' in the PPP (presentation-practice-production) lesson structure, it satisfies the need for a lesson planning template that enshrines a tight logic – and one that finds some validation in skill learning theory, i.e. the theory that declarative knowledge (knowledge-*that*) becomes proceduralized (i.e. converted to knowledge-*how*) through practice. Moreover, the use of guided discovery procedures in order to encourage learners to work out the rules themselves confers a degree of agency on learners that earlier methods, such as the Oral Method, lacked.

On the other hand, the somewhat rigid lesson format of the situational approach, with its emphasis on the accurate reproduction of pre-selected patterns, along with the artificially contrived contexts for presentation, is not a huge advance on the **Audiolingual Method** (see chapter **6**), with which it shares many beliefs about learning and language.

What's in it for us?

In the light of recent developments in educational theory, which argue that all learning is 'situated' (Lave & Wenger 1991), it may be time to revisit the Situational Approach as originally conceived, i.e. where the situation is not simply a context (or pretext) for presenting grammar, but is the central organizing principle in course design. This is particularly relevant now that digital technologies have effectively dissolved the borders between the classroom and 'real life' situations. For example, mobile devices allow learners to record interactions in the outside world for later analysis in the classroom, such as exploring the ways that language choices and the 'context of situation' impact on one another. And corpus linguistics now provides increasingly more detailed descriptions of the kind of language that is used in specific situations – not just the vocabulary and grammar, but the particular features of register and style. The way that language varies according to situation suggests that, in the end, all language use is 'specific', and that language teaching, therefore, is preparing learners to use language for 'specific purposes'.

Alexander, L.G. (1967) *New Concept English: First Things First (Teacher's Book)*. Harlow: Longman.

Billows, L.F. (1961) *The Techniques of Language Teaching*. London: Longmans.

Corder, S.P. (1966) *The Visual Element in Language Teaching*. London: Longmans.

Halliday, M.A.K. (1985) *Introduction to Functional Grammar*. London: Edward Arnold.

Lave, J., & Wenger, E. (1991). *Situated Learning: Legitimate Peripheral Participation*. New York: Cambridge University Press.

Mackey, W.F. (1978) Divorcing language from life: non-contextual linguistics in language teaching. In Strevens, P. (ed.) *In honour of A.S. Hornby*. Oxford: Oxford University Press.

Malinowski, B. (1923) The problem of meaning in primitive languages. Appendix to Ogden, C.K., & Richards, I.A. *The Meaning of Meaning*. London: Routledge & Kegan Paul.

O'Neill, R. (1970) *English in Situations*. Oxford: Oxford University Press.

15 Communicative Language Teaching

> In 1994, H.D. Brown posed the question 'Is there a currently recognised approach that is a generally accepted norm in the field?' and he answered it by saying, 'the answer is a qualified yes. That qualified yes can be captured in the term *communicative language teaching* (CLT)'. A quarter of a century later, the answer is still 'yes', and still qualified.

The background

In the early 1960s, the terms 'communication' and 'communicative' were all the rage. Communication had been invoked as a tool for post-war reconstruction; mass media were now being credited with turning the word into a 'global village'. Driven by innovations in technology, university courses on 'communication studies' and 'communication sciences' proliferated. To sell anything or to get votes, 'communication skills' were considered essential. At the same time, a new branch of linguistics was emerging: sociolinguists were training their sights on the relationship between language and society, interested less in language as an abstract system and more in how it is put to use in actual communication.

It was in this intellectual climate, in 1966, that Dell Hymes put forward the idea of 'communicative competence', i.e. 'competence as to when to speak, when not, and as to what to talk about with whom, when, where, in what manner' (Hymes 1972). Communicative competence, it followed, involves more than having a command of the sum of the grammatical structures that were enshrined in the typical syllabuses of the time. It involves being sensitive to the effect on language choices of such contextual factors as the purpose of the exchange and relation between the participants. Communicative competence was to become the 'big idea' that would underpin Communicative Language Teaching (CLT) and give it its name.

How this big idea might revitalize language teaching was the driving force behind the Council of Europe Modern Languages Project that was launched at Rüschlikon, Switzerland, in 1971, and which effectively marked the inception of CLT. It came to fruition a few years later with the publication of a number of courses based not on a syllabus of grammatical structures but on a syllabus of communicative functions – such as making requests, complaining, narrating and so on. As an epigraph to one of the first of these courses, *Strategies* (Abbs, et al. 1975) the writers quoted David Wilkins (1976), a consultant on the Council of Europe project, to the effect that:

> what people want to do through language is more important than the mastery of language as an unapplied system.

How does it work?

In the teachers' guide to the same series, the authors spell out their approach (Abbs & Freebairn 1979):

> If emphasis is placed on learning a language for communicative purposes, the methods used to promote learning should reflect this. […] A communicative methodology will therefore encourage students to practise language in pairs and groups, where they have equal opportunity to ask, answer, initiate and respond. The teacher assumes a counselling role, initiating activity, listening, helping and advising. Students are encouraged to communicate effectively rather than merely to produce grammatically correct forms of English.

By realigning the goals of instruction away from grammatical accuracy and towards fluency (however defined), and by making a strong commitment to experiential learning, i.e. that communication is best acquired by communicating, the quality and quantity of classroom interaction was set to change radically.

There was still the problem of the syllabus, however. The Council of Europe had urged the adoption of functional-notional syllabuses, i.e. syllabuses made up of items such as *requesting, making comparisons, narrating, duration*. Others argued for a task-based syllabus. Either way, allegiance to the grammar syllabus – on the grounds that grammar items are more generalizable, easier to sequence, and, of course, easier to test – was unshakeable.

And, since grammar items are not easily learned by experience, the 'fluency first' teaching cycle that had originally been proposed, in which learners communicate to the best of their ability, and then get feedback, was sidelined and re-packaged as **Task-based Language Teaching** (see chapter **16**). It was replaced by a less deep-end version of CLT, in which *pre-communicative activities* (typically with a structural focus) precede *communicative activities*. Effectively, the PPP model inherited from **Situational Language Teaching** (see chapter **14**) was dusted off and stretched a little, so as to include more production activities (such as information-gap tasks, role plays and discussions) but not a lot else changed.

For example, the unit structure of a coursebook series that claims to incorporate 'the best features of proven and familiar communicative methodologies' (McCarthy et al. 2005) follows this order:

- Lesson A presents the main grammar point of the unit with some relevant new vocabulary …
- Lesson B teaches the main vocabulary of the unit and builds on the grammar taught in lesson A …
- Lesson C teaches a *Conversation strategy* and some common expressions useful in conversation, followed by a listening activity reinforcing this conversational language …
- Lesson D, after the first three units, focuses on reading and writing skills while providing additional listening and speaking activities.

By the time English language teaching became a global industry in the 1980s and 1990s, it was this 'weak' version of CLT that was taken to be the default form. In many EFL contexts there was no 'communicative revolution' at all.

Does it work?

If widespread adoption is any indication of effectiveness, then CLT – especially in its weak form – would seem to have worked. Most teachers, teacher educators, publishers and institutions subscribe, in principle, at least, to 'being communicative'. What this means is not always clear, but there seems to be a general commitment to the idea that fluency is at least as important as accuracy, that language is a skill as much as a system, and that the goal of second language learning is communicative competence, rather than native-like mastery.

However, CLT has not been without its critics. Resistance to CLT in many (especially non-Western) contexts is argued on the grounds that it might not be appropriate in cultures where theoretical knowledge is valued more highly than practical skills, and where accuracy, not fluency, is the goal of language education. Moreover, a method that prioritizes communicative competence would seem to favour teachers who are themselves communicatively competent, which in many – perhaps most – EFL contexts is not necessarily the case.

What's in it for us?

The lasting legacy of CLT is the idea of the 'communicative activity'. That is to say, an activity in which there is a genuine exchange of meanings, and where participants can use any communicative means at their disposal. In other words, they are not restricted to the use of a pre-specified grammar item. Whether or not a programme consisting solely of such activities enables language acquisition has been thrown into doubt by research suggesting that a 'focus on form' – such as attending to features of the grammar – is necessary. But such activities have made classrooms more interesting, and even fun.

Abbs, B., Ayton, A., & Freebairn, I. (1975) *Strategies: Students' Book*. London: Longman.

Abbs, B., & Freebairn, I. (1979) *Building Strategies: Teacher's Book*. London: Longman.

Brown, H.D. (1994) *Teaching by Principles: An Interactive Approach to Language Pedagogy*. Upper Saddle River, NJ: Prentice Hall Regents.

Hymes, D. (1972) On communicative competence. In Pride, J.B. and Holmes, J. (eds) *Sociolinguistics: Selected Readings*. Harmondsworth: Penguin.

McCarthy, M., McCarten, J., & Sandiford, H. (2005) *Touchstone 1 (Teacher's edition)*. Cambridge: Cambridge University Press.

Wilkins, D. (1976) *Notional Syllabuses*. Oxford: Oxford University Press.

16   Task-based Language Teaching

> 'A presentation methodology is based on the belief that out of accuracy comes fluency. A task-based methodology is based on the belief that out of fluency comes accuracy, and that learning is prompted and refined by the need to communicate' (D. Willis 1990).

The background

In 1979, the Regional Institute of English in Bangalore, India, under the guidance of N.S. Prabhu, embarked on a five-year project that was to achieve legendary status in the history of English language teaching. Referred to ever since as 'the Bangalore Project', the aim was to teach English to a small number of classes in local primary and secondary schools using a syllabus that was based – not on a list of grammatical patterns, as was customary in India at the time – but on a series of tasks, where *tasks* are defined by Willis (1996) as 'activities where the target language is used by the learner for a communicative purpose (goal) in order to achieve an outcome'. Dissatisfied with the prevailing 'structural-oral-situational' methodology, but sceptical about replacing a syllabus of grammar items with a syllabus of functions or notions (as some proponents of **Communicative Language Teaching** were advocating – see chapter **15**), Prabhu opted instead for a task-based approach, and for 'the creation of conditions in which learners engage in an effort to cope with communication' (1987).

In this sense, he was following the lead of advocates of a 'strong' form of CLT, such as Dick Allwright (1979) who insisted: 'If the "language teacher's" management activities are directed exclusively at involving the learners in solving communication problems in the target language, then language learning will take care of itself'. In other words, you learn to communicate simply by communicating. And tasks – doing things that involve real language use – provide the ideal context and motivation for communicating. Prabhu, like many after him, rejected the view that a pre-selected syllabus, whether of grammar items or of functions, and the PPP methodology associated with it, are the optimal route to proficiency.

Although supported by a long tradition in progressive education of 'learning by doing', initially TBLT lacked a sound empirical basis. Certainly, research into SLA was starting to cast doubt on the wisdom of teaching according to a syllabus of 'forms' (i.e. grammatical structures). The learner's 'inbuilt' syllabus seemed to be immune to this kind of manipulation. Moreover, research into the interactions between learners when performing tasks, including the way that they negotiate and repair communication breakdowns, suggested that these interactions might be a fertile site for acquisition. On the other hand, evidence from other 'deep-end' learning contexts, such as **immersion** (see chapter 1), indicated that an exclusive focus on communication – without some explicit attention to the formal features of the language (called 'focus on form') – might result in 'arrested development', i.e. the temporary or permanent stabilization of the language system.

Accordingly, the Bangalore model of TBLT – which discouraged 'any sustained attention to language itself' (Prabhu 1987) – was reconfigured by scholars such as Mike Long so as to include a focus on form. But it is a focus on form 'which is by definition reactive, i.e. responsive to the learner's current stage of development' (Long 2015). In other words, 'students lead, the teacher follows'.

How does it work?

Much ink has been shed as to what constitutes a task, but there is general agreement that a task should be directed at achieving some outcome, where language is the means but not the end. Filling in the verbs in a gap-fill exercise is not a task. Finding the differences in two pictures, by exchanging spoken descriptions with your partner, is. As is the collaborative planning and taking of a class photo. Tasks can involve any one of the four skills, together or in isolation. They are more often done collaboratively, but they can be done individually, and in class or on line.

The selection and sequencing of tasks is more problematic, since it is not always clear in what ways one task is more difficult than another, or in what way tasks may build on one another to form a coherent learning sequence. A series of projects – or one continuous project, such as the design and maintenance of a class website – offer possible ways of structuring a course. Attempts to sequence tasks according to the grammatical forms that they are likely to require have been dismissed as task-*supported* learning, and not the real thing.

There are various suggested models of how a task-based lesson can be designed. Prabhu himself favoured beginning with the teacher performing the task, and then the learners following suit. Jane Willis (1996) reverses this sequence, so that viewing the skilled performance of the task occurs *after* learners have attempted it themselves (and reported on the outcomes). At some post-task stage, attention might be devoted to how the task performance could be improved, including an explicit focus on form.

Does it work?

While the (somewhat delayed) evaluation of the Bangalore project was itself inconclusive, there is probably no method that has been more persuasively championed than TBLT: it comes supported by an ever-growing research base into SLA, especially the school of SLA that subscribes to a cognitive view of learning, i.e. one that construes the learner as a 'limited capacity information processor'. Performing tasks, and getting feedback on them, would seem to optimize this kind of processing. Laboratory-type studies of specific features of the method, such as different ways of focusing on form, have been encouraging. Evidence that alternative models of instruction – such as PPP – work any better is scarce.

Why isn't TBLT more widely applied, then? One reason might be the syllabusing issue, mentioned above. There is also the plausible concern that, without a language syllabus, learners will simply recycle their existing (limited) competences. More acute still is the uncertainty, on the part of many teachers and their supervisors, as to how to deal with the unpredictability of task outcomes. Not to mention the actual management challenges of setting up, monitoring and providing feedback on pair and group work. Where TBLT seems to work best is when experienced teachers are working with smallish groups of learners, e.g. immigrants, whose practical language needs can be accurately predicted, such that the programme can be designed to address them.

What's in it for us?

The idea that the 'students lead [and] the teacher follows' is a powerful one – implying a fundamental redistribution of power in the curriculum. Taken to an extreme, it suggests the adoption of what is called a 'process syllabus', that is, a syllabus that is in a constant state of negotiation, as learners' needs emerge, their interests fluctuate and their capacities evolve. In this sense, 'tasks are not isolated events but parts of a process whose goals are determined by the interaction between learners and their expressed interests and needs' (Legutke & Thomas 1991). Recent developments in some mainstream education systems, e.g. Finland, where school subjects are no longer taught as independent disciplines, but are merged into the collaborative implementation of long-term projects involving a whole constellation of tasks, might seem to offer a way forward.

Allwright, R. (1979) Language learning through communication practice. In Brumfit, C. & Johnson, K. (eds) *The Communicative Approach to Language Teaching*. Oxford: Oxford University Press.

Legutke, M., & Thomas, H. (1991) *Process and Experience in the Language Classroom*. Harlow: Longman.

Long, M. (2015) *Second Language Acquisition and Task-Based Language Teaching*. Oxford: Wiley Blackwell.

Prabhu, N.S. (1987) *Second Language Pedagogy*. Oxford: Oxford University Press.

Willis, D. (1990) *The Lexical Syllabus: A New Approach to Language Teaching*. London: Collins.

Willis, J. (1996) *A Framework for Task-Based Learning*. Harlow: Longman.

17   Competency-based Teaching

> In formulating the syllabus prescriptions for CLT, van Ek (1975/1980) argued that 'language-learning objectives, like other learning objectives, are defined in terms of *behaviour*. The aim of learning is always to enable the learner to do something which he [or she] could not do at the beginning of the learning process'. Competency-based Teaching takes this principle to its logical extreme.

The background

In principle, a communicative approach focuses less on what learners *know* about the language than what they can *do* with it. It follows, therefore, that a curriculum whose goals are defined in terms of *competencies* – that is, the specific skills that learners will be able to do – is more functional than one that is based around a list of discrete items of grammar.

Competency-based Teaching, then, starts with an analysis of the specific behaviours – or skills – that are needed to do a job, to pursue a field of study, or to survive as a tourist, for example. These skills (sometimes called *key competencies* or even *life skills*) form the basis of the course design, and are the goals – or *outcomes* – of classroom instruction and testing. Competencies are often expressed in the form of *can do statements,* probably the best known of which (for language teaching) are those that were devised for the Common European Framework of Reference for Languages: Learning, Teaching, Assessment (CEFR). For example, here are the self-assessment descriptors for the skill of writing at A1, A2 and B1 levels (Council of Europe 2001):

	A1	**A2**	**B1**
WRITING	I can write a short, simple postcard, for example sending holiday greetings. I can fill in forms with personal details, for example entering my name, nationality and address on a hotel registration form.	I can write short, simple notes and messages relating to matters in areas of immediate need. I can write a very simple personal letter, for example thanking someone for something.	I can write simple connected text on topics which are familiar or of personal interest. I can write personal letters describing experiences and impressions.

These very broad outcomes can be specified in yet finer detail: the finer the better, arguably, since discrete outcomes are more efficiently taught and tested than very general ones. A case in point is the Pearson Global Scale of English (GSE) which boasts over 1,800 *can do* statements.

How does it work?

If a method is defined – not just by its syllabus, materials and procedures – but also by its goals, then Competency-based Teaching certainly merits consideration as a method in its own right. It is not so clear, though, as to how the syllabus goals are to be met. As the CEFR (Council of Europe 2001) insists, 'such statements of learning objectives say nothing about the processes by which learners come to be able to act in the required ways … They say nothing about the ways in which teachers facilitate the processes of language acquisition and learning'. Nevertheless, the fact that the goals of learning are typically expressed in terms of abilities (as in the *can do* statements), rather than as grammar or vocabulary items, suggests that a skills-based approach would be appropriate. Such an approach would be one in which the specific behavioural goal – e.g. 'writing a short personal letter' – is modelled for the learners, and then practised by them until it is sufficiently 'automated'.

However, as in the case of the CEFR, attempts to flesh out the descriptors by specifying the precise linguistic elements (e.g. the grammar and vocabulary) that are implicated in each competence may undermine a skills-based approach, inviting a more traditional, atomistic teaching approach, along the lines of the PPP (present-practice-produce) model (see chapter **14**). More problematic still is the fact that, whatever methodology is employed, a key component of the teaching-learning cycle is testing to see if the target competencies have been acquired. And the more precisely and narrowly the competencies are defined, the more items there will be to test.

Does it work?

Critics of a competency-based approach argue that its narrowly-specified, utilitarian goals artificially constrain learning, producing learners with a narrow range of competencies and few transferrable skills. They also argue that the reduction of learning into discrete, modularized chunks distorts the nature of language and language use in the real world. As Auerbach (1986) comments, 'the focus on a bottom-up, building block pedagogy may produce such a narrow dissection into sub-units that students cannot see the forest for the trees'.

The trend to 'commodify' learning in this way is consistent with the way that education is increasingly being construed as a business, where production targets and marketing plans directly determine the way that the work-force is trained, and where managers (and teachers) are accountable both to their stakeholders and to their customers. As Gray and Block (2012) put it, 'terms such as "outcomes", "value added", "knowledge transfer", "the knowledge economy" and above all "accountability" have become part of the day-to-day vocabulary of education'.

Worse still, accountability encourages a culture of continuous testing. As Diane Ravitch (2010) complains – with reference to the introduction of 'common core standards' into the US education system – 'How did testing and accountability become the main levers of school reform? … What was once an effort to improve the quality of education turned into an accounting strategy'. And she adds, 'Tests should follow the curriculum. They should not replace it or precede it' (ibid.).

What's in it for us?

Despite its business-like associations, the idea that the curriculum should be 'reverse engineered' according to an analysis of learners' needs is not necessarily an unworthy one. In fact, it is a fundamental principle underpinning the teaching of ESP: the starting point of course design is a needs analysis, from which the course objectives, materials and even teaching procedures are derived. Success of the programme is measured in terms of how well the needs have been met.

Moreover, it is a fact that, as Heyworth (2004) argues (in favour of the CEFR) 'all knowledge of language is partial'. He adds that 'the concept of partial competencies reinforces the need for negotiation of objectives with learners, and recognition of the fact that not everyone has to set off on the journey to learn the whole of the language. Learning a language is not an "all or nothing" undertaking'. This is a view that acknowledges the widespread plurilingualism and mobility associated with globalization, where conformity to native-speaker models of proficiency is of less utility than communicative resourcefulness. This suggests that a competency-based model – but one that is negotiated in much the same way that a process syllabus is negotiated (see chapter **16 Task-based Language Teaching**) and one that, above all, is not over-burdened with continuous testing – might well serve the needs of learners in an increasingly globalized world.

Auerbach, E. (1986) Competency-based ESL: one step forward or two steps back? *TESOL Quarterly*, 20: 411–430.

Council of Europe (2001) *Common European Framework of Reference for Languages: Learning, Teaching, Assessment.* Cambridge: Cambridge University Press.

Gray, J., & Block, D. (2012) The marketisation of language teacher education and neoliberalism: characteristics, consequences and future prospects. In Block, D., Gray, J., & Holborow, M. (eds) *Neoliberalism and Applied Linguistics.* London: Routledge.

Heyworth, F. (2004) Why the CEF is important. In Morrow, K. (ed.) *Insights from the Common European Framework.* Oxford: Oxford University Press.

Ravitch, D. (2010) *The Death and Life of the Great American School System: How Testing and Choice are Undermining Education.* New York: Basic Books.

van Ek, J. (1975/1980) *Threshold Level English.* Oxford: Pergamon.

18 Whole Language Learning

The history of methods is a history of polar opposites: learning vs acquisition, product vs process, accuracy vs fluency – and teaching 'bits' of language vs engaging with whole texts. Whole Language Learning aims to gather together the second of each of these polarities.

The background

In the 1920s, the French schoolteacher Célestin Freinet promoted what he called a 'work-based pedagogy' that rejected the kind of centralized school-planning associated with textbooks and examinations. His best known innovation was the introduction of a printing press into his school, so pupils could generate their own materials, including a school magazine, which they exchanged with pupils at a sister school. Freinet was impelled by the belief that 'the key features of empty academic activity are rules, books and teachers … all forcing pupils to produce work with absolutely no basis in real life' (quoted in Clandfield and Sivell 1990). Instead, 'by re-establishing the cycle of life, by assuring constant motivation through creative work, we get beyond dry academic exercises and reach a far superior form of classroom activity'.

Freinet occupies one end of a continuum along which all teachers – whether teachers of first language literacy or of an additional language – situate themselves. At one extreme, there are those who believe that you learn a language by studying each of its components first, that is, by progressing from the parts to the whole (often by means of 'dry academic exercises'). And there are those (like Freinet) who believe that you learn the components of the language by engaging with it as an integrated whole, in the form, for example, of 'creative work'. That is, learning goes from whole to part.

In first language literacy teaching, this division is most famously represented in the arguments (often acrimonious) between those who advocate the teaching of phonics and those who don't. Phonics is the study of sound-letter relationships, and its proponents argue that using this knowledge to 'sound out' words is the best way of learning to read. A whole-language approach, on the other hand, takes a 'top-down' perspective, in which reading involves working out word meanings from context, and recognizing word shapes by means of activities such as being read to while following the words on the page, or reading aloud with the assistance of an adult or a slightly more proficient classmate.

The whole language movement was popularized in North America in the 1990s, as a reaction to the prevailing atomistic (or 'building block') approach to curriculum design, in which language arts were taught and tested in discrete, de-contextualized units. Among its core principles are the following (after Freeman & Freeman 1998):

- Learning goes from whole to part.
- Reading, writing, speaking and listening all develop together.
- Lessons should be learner-centred because learning is the active construction of knowledge.
- Learning takes place in social interaction.

The whole language approach emphasizes the social and cultural dimension of education. It also aims to promote the learner's self-realization through learning, a feature that aligns it with the humanistic tradition of education. In this sense 'whole' stands not only for 'whole language', but also 'whole person': learning works best when the learner is engaged not only intellectually but emotionally and even physically.

How does it work?

Whole Language Learning, as implemented in second language classrooms, shares many characteristics of both Task-based and Text-based Instruction. The starting point of any teaching cycle is not a discrete item of grammar, but the performance of a task, or engagement with a text. Only at a later stage in the cycle are specific linguistic features the target of instruction – and only as deemed necessary for the improved performance of the task. This is why Whole Language Learning is most often associated with the teaching of the skills of reading and writing. Marie Wilson Nelson (1991), for example, describes a five-year experiment at a college in the US, where writing workshops were offered to small groups, including English language learners, and where there was no formal writing – or grammar, or vocabulary – instruction. Instead, the students were – in the words of the program publicity – invited to:

- Choose topics that interest you and your group
- Freewrite (i.e. write freely) without worrying about correctness on the first draft
- Revise your freewrites. Your group will help you …
- Learn to copy-edit your writing for publication

Instead of pre-teaching or modelling the skills of writing, a process approach was adopted – i.e. one which involved collaboration and multiple drafts – and in which 'the tutors found that the most acceptable and effective teaching was to give the help the students asked for when they asked for it'– instruction, that is to say, 'at the point of need'.

Does it work?

Nelson (op. cit.) and five independent teams of researchers found so: 'Despite the loss of drive some suffered at first without grades, motivation surged when they experienced writing's rewards: pride of publication …, feelings of accomplishment, influence on others, better grades in other courses, competence, empathy and praise from friends, and … emotional release'. Likewise, 'free voluntary reading', an approach to first language literacy training that is energetically promoted by Stephen Krashen (2004), and which is entirely consistent with the principles of Whole Language Learning, is equally positively evaluated: 'In-school free reading studies and "out of school" self-reported free voluntary reading studies show that more reading results in better reading comprehension, writing style, vocabulary, spelling, and grammatical development'. And he adds, 'in face-to-face comparisons, reading is consistently shown to be more efficient than direct instruction'. Krashen argues that the approach applies equally well to second language development.

What's in it for us?

Despite these enthusiastic claims, as teachers we might be advised to hedge our bets – especially given the research evidence that endorses the value of a 'focus on form' (see chapter **16 Task-based Language Teaching**). As an instance of how a compromise might be reached, Courtney Cazden (1992) argues for what she calls *whole language plus*: 'As people of any age learn to read and write, they need help in focusing attention on specific features of written language'. So, even when the primary focus is on task performance, e.g. fluent reading or writing, she argues for the need for 'instructional detours' in order to shift attention, when necessary, away from the whole and on to the parts: 'The idea of a detour preserves what I believe to be essential: the prior establishment of a main road of meaningful language use, to which the detour is a momentary diversion when needed'. This is entirely consistent with Nelson's notion of instruction 'at the point of need' or with what others have called 'just in time teaching'. It is an approach that Freinet, with his printing press, would have approved of.

Cazden, C. (1992) *Whole Language Plus: Essays on Literacy in the US and NZ*. New York: Teachers College Press.

Clandfield, D., & Sivell, J. (eds.) (1990) *Co-operative Learning and Social Change: Selected Writings of Célestin Freinet*. Montréal: Our Schools, Our Selves.

Freeman, Y.S., & Freeman, D.E. (1998) *ESL/EFL Teaching: Principles for Success*. Heinemann.

Krashen, S.D. (2004) *The Power of Reading: Insights from the Research (2nd edition)*. Portsmouth, NH: Heinemann.

Nelson, M.W. (1991) *At the Point of Need: Teaching Basic and ESL Writers*. Portsmouth, NH: Heinemann.

19   Content-based Instruction

> Content-based Instruction takes the principle of immersion and applies it – not to life in its totality – but to the school context in particular.

The background

On October 30, 1963, in a living room near Montreal, Canada, a dozen concerned parents of English-speaking children met to discuss what could be done about the lamentable state of their children's French. As a solution, they proposed a form of language immersion, in which the children would be taught their school subjects (or some of them), not in their first language, English, but in French. This was a radical idea at the time, when bilingualism was still regarded with deep suspicion: the popular view was that the influence of the second language would retard development of the first language, not to mention the negative effects it would have on education in general. But, with the support of experts at McGill University in Montreal, the first class of Anglophone children to be taught in French was set up at kindergarten level in September 1965. By 1983, the Canadian Immersion Program was providing over 100,000 Anglophone children with at least some part of their regular curriculum in French; five years later this figure had more than doubled, and the idea had spread to the United States, where immersion programs in Spanish led the way.

That living room meeting in Montreal in 1963 planted a seed that would give rise to a wide variety of educational options – and a steady trickle of acronyms – that, in various ways, combined content teaching and language learning. These include CBI (content-based instruction – a term more commonly used in the US), CLIL (content and language integrated learning – originally a European term) and EMI (English-medium instruction – more commonly used with reference to tertiary education). The basic principle underlying all these different versions of classroom immersion is that an additional language can be acquired when that language is being used as the vehicle of instruction, even if the learner's attention is primarily, although not exclusively, on the message and not on the medium.

Of course, learning school subjects in a language that is not the home language is not a novelty: for centuries it was standard practice in Western Europe to be schooled in Latin, for example, and classical Arabic is still the medium of instruction in many Muslim countries nowadays. During the period of European colonization of countries such as India, Brazil or Mexico education was typically mediated in the language of the colonizers. And few children of immigrants today have any choice but to be educated in the language of their 'host' country, despite UN recommendations that early learning should be conducted in the home language wherever possible.

How does it work?

The defining characteristic of the content-based classroom is that the syllabus is organized around content, not grammar. Typically, the content will be the subjects of the school curriculum – geography, PT, art, history etc. These subjects will be taught in the target language – English, in the case of English-medium instruction. The relative importance that is then given to the code, i.e. the features of the language – its grammar, vocabulary and pronunciation – seems to depend as much on the whim of individual teachers as on the specific method that is being followed. But, as in Task-based Learning, there has been a shift in emphasis from content only to content-*plus*-code in recent years. In immersion teaching as first practised in Canada, little or no formal attention was paid to the code: teachers simply taught their subjects in French, but allowed learners to ask questions and respond in their L1. Proponents of CLIL, on the other hand, are insistent that due attention should be given to the code, such as pre-teaching the vocabulary and grammar that the learners will need, and providing explicit error correction. Either way, it seems that successful teachers of Content-based Instruction are able to do the following:

- grade their classroom language to ensure comprehensibility, and/or use the learners' first language when necessary;
- use multiple modes (e.g. graphics as well as language) to help construct the meaning of the texts the students will read or listen to;

- scaffold the learners' interactions by asking strategically-placed questions that guide learners to a deeper understanding of texts, and a more articulate expression of their own meanings;
- provide unambiguous feedback on learners' output, and
- continuously assess learners' evolving understanding of the subject matter, as well as their control of the vehicular language.

Does it work?

The Canadian experience shows that French immersion students develop higher levels of fluency and comprehension than those studying French as a curriculum subject (e.g. for an hour a day) and – importantly – their academic success is not prejudiced by studying school subjects in French. On the contrary, the bi- or multilingualism that results is both a personal and a social asset. However, this situation is somewhat exceptional. For a start, these learners' first language (English) is sufficiently supported at home and in their community, which is seldom, if ever, the case for children of immigrants or other minority groups. Moreover, the Canadian immersion teachers are fluent speakers of the vehicular language, whereas in many CLIL contexts teachers may be less than fully proficient in the language of instruction.

But even the Canadian learners do not always achieve native-like levels of proficiency in French, a fact that has been attributed to, among other things, lack of explicit instruction and corrective feedback. These are exactly the areas that a CLIL methodology claims to remedy, by providing balanced attention to both code and content – what Roy Lyster (2007) calls 'a counter-balanced approach'. Whether, in fact, it does this depends on a variety of factors, not least the skills of the teacher, their training, and their beliefs. On the whole, however, research into CLIL suggests that, in the right conditions and given sufficient attention to the formal features of the vehicular language, the L2 learning outcomes are positive, even if not perfect. Less thoroughly researched are the effects on overall academic achievement, and advocates of CLIL will need to work hard to convince doubting parents in some CLIL contexts – e.g. where the standard of subject matter teaching is not already strong – that their children are getting the integrated education that CLIL promises.

What's in it for us?

The foregrounding of subject matter knowledge – e.g. geography, science or art – solves the problem that has plagued second language teaching for centuries – i.e. that it is a discipline with no real content. In the absence of a subject, the language itself, or its literature, tends to become the subject, and a great deal of classroom time is devoted to studying grammar or reading the 'classics'. But Content-based Instruction fulfils the promise of communicative language teaching: that – in Brumfit's (2001) words – 'we may learn the tokens of language formally, but we learn the system by using it through reading or writing, or conversing'. Content-based Instruction gives us something to read, write and converse *about*.

Brumfit, C. (2001) *Individual Freedom in Language Teaching: Helping Learners to Develop a Dialect of their Own*. Oxford: Oxford University Press.

Lyster, R. (2007) *Learning and Teaching Languages Through Content: A Counterbalanced Approach*. Amsterdam: John Benjamins.

20 Dogme ELT/ Teaching Unplugged

> 'The language I learn in the classroom is a communal product derived through a jointly constructed process', wrote Michael Breen in 1985. 'Dogme' teachers have adopted this idea as their … dogma!

The background

In 1995, over a bottle of red wine, the Danish film-maker Lars von Trier and three colleagues drafted the manifesto of the Dogme 95 film-makers collective. They were driven by a commitment to rescue cinema from big-budget, hi-tech, Hollywood-style production values and to recover what von Trier referred to as 'our joyful film-making'. In order to make films that would be true to the 'inner story' of the characters, the group pledged allegiance to a set of 'vows', the first of which was:

> Shooting should be done on location. Props and sets must not be brought in (if a particular prop is necessary for the story, a location must be chosen where the prop is to be found).

By analogy, in 2000, I wrote a short, intentionally provocative, article (Thornbury 2000) suggesting the need for a similar rescue action in ELT, which – at least in the contexts I was familiar with – seemed to be drowning in an embarrassment of riches. An over-dependence on manufactured materials (I argued) ran counter to the often expressed desire of both teachers and learners to create more opportunities for real language use in their classrooms. This was partly due to the single-minded fixation of published materials (such as coursebooks) on teaching the system (mainly grammar) rather than on engaging learners in applying the system to create meanings for themselves – which had been a core tenet of the **Communicative Approach** (see chapter **15**). There was also a growing reliance on – and uncritical enthusiasm for – the use of technological aids, such as interactive whiteboards and mobile phones, but without any apparent improvement in the quality of classroom interaction.

In the same style and spirit as the Dogme filmmakers' vows, I drafted some vows of my own, the first being:

> Teaching should be done using only the resources that teachers and students bring to the classroom – i.e. themselves – and whatever happens to be in the classroom. If a particular piece of material is necessary for the lesson, a location must be chosen where that material is to be found (e.g. library, resource centre, bar, students' club …).

The article stimulated the formation of an online discussion group, *Dogme ELT* (but later re-labelled as *Teaching unplugged*). Out of this ongoing discussion, a number of principles emerged that teachers sympathetic to this approach seemed to hold in common, irrespective of the contexts they were teaching in. These might be summarised as being:

- Learning is a social and dialogic process, where knowledge is co-constructed rather than transmitted or imported from teacher/coursebook to learner.
- Learning can be mediated through talk, especially talk that is shaped and supported (i.e. scaffolded) by the teacher.
- Materials-mediated teaching is the 'scenic' route to learning, but the direct route is located in the interactivity between teachers and learners, and between the learners themselves.
- The content most likely to engage learners and to trigger learning processes is that which is already there, supplied by the 'people in the room'.
- Rather than being acquired, language (including grammar) emerges: it is an organic process that occurs given the right conditions.
- The teacher's primary function, apart from establishing the kind of classroom dynamic which encourages learner interaction, is to optimise language learning affordances, by, for example, directing attention to features of the emergent language.
- Providing space for the learner's voice means accepting that the learner's beliefs, knowledge, experiences, concerns and desires are valid content in the language classroom.

In a book published nearly a decade later (Meddings & Thornbury 2009), these principles were pared down to just three core precepts:

- Dogme is about teaching that is *conversation-driven*.
- Dogme is about teaching that is *materials-light*.
- Dogme is about teaching that focuses on *emergent language*.

How does it work?

In principle, Dogme ELT shares many characteristics of **Task-based Language Teaching** (see chapter **16**), and is arguably a 'minimalist' form of it. It rejects a curriculum based on a syllabus of 'forms', but prefers a process syllabus, i.e. one that is continuously negotiated by the learners; it adopts a 'fluency-first' pedagogy (on the assumption that accuracy is late-acquired); it advocates a reactive (as opposed to a pro-active) focus on form 'at the point of need', that is to say, corrective feedback or grammar explanations or vocabulary input are provided at the moment when the need for such a focus arises during task performance. A typical teaching sequence might begin with a classroom discussion around a topic that a learner has volunteered – or may have been tasked to prepare for – out of which the teacher will extract some relevant language items that might, in turn, be recycled in a follow-up writing task.

In practice, a Dogme approach will vary according to its context. For some teachers and in some situations, it may be enough to intersperse their teaching with 'Dogme moments', such as when a learner's utterance offers a learning opportunity and the lesson takes a brief detour in pursuit of it. Assuming they are in a context where they are allowed to, other teachers may be motivated to design their whole course according to Dogme principles.

Does it work?

Dogme is under-researched, but its critics have identified some possible weaknesses. For a start, it seems to favour small groups of motivated learners who are prepared to 'suspend disbelief' in a programme that has no clear syllabus nor coursebook. Moreover, because its approach is essentially reactive, it assumes its teachers have the skills – and the language – to deal spontaneously with learners' output. And the fact that the emphasis is on conversation as the context out of which language 'emerges' means that learners may be less well prepared for more formal or written registers, such as academic writing. Finally, Dogme is open to the same charge as Task-based Instruction – that the lack of a syllabus of preselected language items means that learners are simply relying on their existing competence without being pushed to extend it. In response, proponents of a Dogme approach appeal to sociocultural theories of learning, which suggest that development can occur through collaborative activity, especially when 'scaffolded' by a supportive teacher.

What's in it for us?

Despite the above criticisms, many teachers have felt liberated when their lessons are no longer shackled to coursebook texts or a preselected 'grammar point'. In fact, research into teachers' developmental trajectories suggests that many expert teachers learn to rely less on 'imported' materials and more on what arises from the learners themselves. At the same time, learners who have experienced greater control of the classroom topic agenda typically rate 'Dogme moments' highly. Apart from anything else, 'doing a Dogme lesson' from time to time might be a very productive professional development exercise – a fact attested by many teachers who choose this option as part of their 'experimental practice' on in-service teacher education courses.

Breen, M. (1985) The social context for language learning – a neglected situation? *Studies in Second Language Acquisition*, 7: 135–158.

Meddings, L., & Thornbury, S. (2009) *Teaching Unplugged: Dogme in English Language Teaching*. Peaslake, Surrey: Delta Publishing.

Thornbury, S. (2000) A dogma for EFL. *IATEFL Issues*, 153: 2.

D: Visionaries

Each of these methods is closely associated with its architect, who, in each case, had a unique, even mystical vision of teaching, often combined with a charismatic teaching style. Nevertheless, some of the practices associated with these methods have been co-opted into more mainstream methodology, even if the beliefs that underpin them have not.

Community Language Learning

> The anxiety and identity dislocation that so often comes
> with adopting a second language might better be treated –
> not by a teacher – but by a psychotherapist. Or a teacher-
> therapist. That, at least, is the thinking that underpins
> *Community language learning*.

The background

> When I hear my voice, I just hate it … It is not simply that my ears hate
> my mouth, or my mouth hates my eyes. The inner conflict inhabits
> my entire being. This makes me feel that my own 'self' is falling apart.
> Now I have two 'mes' inside myself. A 'me' with whom I am familiar
> and with whom I feel connected … The other 'me' is a stranger.

Thus, Zhou Wu (1993, quoted in Granger 2004) recalls the anxiety and
loss of identity associated with migrating to Canada and discovering
that his English, which seemed perfectly adequate at home in China,
failed him in the Canadian context.

Zhou Wu might have benefitted from Community language learning
(CLL, also known as *Counselling-learning*). Developed in the 1960s
and 1970s by Charles Curran, a Jesuit priest and practising counsellor,
CLL imports into language instruction the kind of three-step exchange
that is fundamental to non-directive, client-centred and 'whole person'
counselling practices. In this exchange, the 'client' articulates his or her
fears, anxieties, or desires in language that is often highly-charged and
emotional. The counsellor paraphrases (or reflects back) the content
of the client's utterance in language which is more detached, more
matter-of-fact, which the client, in turn, is invited to repeat. In this way,
the client comes to view their situation more objectively, to gain some
control over it, and, eventually, to become less reliant on the counsellor.
Curran's insight was that this sort of twin-code communication of
emotional talk and rational talk, in which the words of one register

are 'translated' into another, could be successfully adapted to language teaching, especially if conducted in the kind of mutually supportive community context associated with group therapy.

Hence *community* language learning – because Curran's other insight was that language is not simply a means of communication, but that it plays a vital role in building and maintaining communities – even communities as small and as artificially constituted as a group of language learners. This means that the language should not be imposed on the learners, in the form, for example, of a syllabus and coursebook, but that it should emerge jointly from them, and simply be translated for them by the teacher-counsellor.

How does it work?

The classic CLL procedure is one in which small groups of learners (also known as 'clients'), seated in a circle, jointly construct a conversation on a topic of their own devising, with the unobtrusive assistance of the teacher (or 'knower').

Any student can start, and there is no set order or even requirement to participate. A student quietly tells the teacher, in her L1, what she wants to say in the L2. The teacher translates. The student repeats and the teacher may correct if necessary. When the student is satisfied, the utterance is recorded. Other students respond, each utterance being assembled, fine-tuned and recorded in turn. Here, for example, is the conversation that three adult Spanish learners of English constructed:

S1: Emma, where are you going tonight?
S2: Tonight I am going to have supper out.
S3: Where are you going to have supper?
S2: I don't know. I am being taken out.
S1: Who are you going with?
S2: I'm going with, with a guy, but he isn't my boyfriend.
S1: And where is your boyfriend?
S2: Do you mean now?
S1: No, not now. Where will he be this evening?
S2: He's going to play water polo.
S3: Hmm, water polo. Very interesting. Is your boyfriend hunky?
S2: Yes, he's very hunky.

The teacher replays the whole recording, and chooses elements of it to transcribe on to the board in order to draw attention to particular linguistic features that are considered to be within the learners' current learning capability. Other activities might complement this basic framework, such as reading the text aloud, as well as reflecting on the experience itself.

Does it work?

Even in its heyday, CLL was seldom subject to exhaustive methods comparison studies, and most of the success its proponents claim for it is largely anecdotal. It is perfectly plausible, however, that a strong group dynamic could develop using CLL procedures, and that this in turn could be a powerful motivator. Moreover, the freedom to control the classroom discourse is likely to be welcomed by more assertive and independent learners. Research (e.g. Slimani 1989) into more conventional methods suggests that, when learners have some say in the choice of topics, then 'uptake' (i.e. what the learners remember from the lesson) is enhanced. However, the impracticality of adopting CLL in most learning contexts militates against it: classes need to be small, the teacher needs to be proficient in the learners' L1, and capable of dealing with linguistic issues spontaneously and at the point of need. (In this sense, CLL shares many of the challenges of **Dogme ELT**, see chapter 20.) It is perhaps best employed as a source of specific techniques, rather than as a method in its own right.

What's in it for us?

Stripped of its quasi-mystical rhetoric – e.g. 'an incarnate-redemptive learning experience' (Curran 1983) – CLL still has a lot to offer, not least in its foregrounding of socially-oriented collaborative learning. This is in line with learning theories (such as Vygotsky's sociocultural learning) of which Curran, in his time, would have been unaware. It is also consistent with the view that the classroom has its own unique 'culture' with its own dynamic and momentum. As Michael Breen (1985) notes: 'Whether or not the teacher plans a lesson in advance, the actual working out of that lesson in the class demands joint endeavour. The lesson-in-process is most often different from that which either the teacher or the learners anticipated before the lesson began'. Community language learning takes this inherent unpredictability and turns it into an opportunity.

It might also be interesting to know what Curran would have made of online social networking and its potential to provide both a context and a motivation for jointly constructed learning opportunities. Sites (such as www.italki.com) that provide a venue for users of different languages to interact and 'teach' one another by, for example, translating and editing each other's texts, offer a possible solution to some of the scale limitations of CLL as first conceived.

Breen, M.P. (1985) The social context for language learning: a neglected situation? *Studies in Second Language Acquisition*, 7: 135–158.

Curran, C. (1983) Counselling-Learning. In Oller, J.W., Richard-Amato, P.A. (eds) *Methods that Work: A Smorgasbord of Ideas for Language Teachers.* Rowley, Mass.: Newbury House.

Granger, C.A. (2004) *Silence in Second Language Learning: A Psychoanalytic Reading.* Cleveland: Multilingual Matters.

Slimani, A. (1989) The role of topicalization in classroom language learning. *System*, 17: 223–234.

Terrence Rattigan's popular comedy *French Without Tears* (1936) was named after a well-known textbook of the time. The title plays on the widespread longing for a language teaching method that is painless, pleasurable, and fast. Suggestopedia claims to be all those things: language learning without tears.

The background

Second language learning is famously slow and time-consuming. Literally hundreds of hours may be needed just to reach intermediate level, especially if the learner has little or no direct contact with speakers of the language. And, since time is money, this constitutes an enormous financial investment for most learners or their sponsors. Any method that offers a significant shortcut to this arduous, expensive and often thankless task will surely triumph. Suggestopedia claims to do exactly that: it increases the speed of learning by as much as 25 times, its practitioners attest. The memorization of 1,000 foreign language words in just an hour is another frequently cited figure.

Its architect and active publicist, Georgi Lozanov (1926–2012) was a Bulgarian scientist and educator who believed that the human mind's capacity for exceptional feats of memory is inhibited only by our need to filter out unconscious and irrational 'noise'. While, for day-to-day purposes, these filters are necessary, they seriously constrain our ability to learn. Lozanov's solution, called *Suggestopedia*, involved unblocking (or 'de-suggesting') the inhibitors that have accumulated over the course of our learning history, while at the same time substituting these with positive suggestions that will massively enhance our future learning potential.

First popularized in the West in the 1970s (in a book that also had chapters on clairvoyance, auras, prophecy, past lives, faith healing, psychokinesis, and talking to plants), Suggestopedia is easy to dismiss as quackery. This negative perception is not helped by the unsubstantiated claims of some of its more fervent advocates: 'Stress and anxiety tend to over-activate the left hemisphere and the sympathetic division of the autonomic nervous system, which reduces receptivity at the paraconscious level. With Lozanov's method, the mind must be soaring high and free' (Hansen 1998).

Nevertheless, the notion that, simply by unlocking our unconscious minds, effortless learning capacities will result, has always had popular appeal. Lozanov's accomplishment was to provide a quasi-scientific veneer to this 'magical thinking', combining techniques from yoga, meditation, hypnotherapy, and music therapy, so as to lull learners into an infantilized but highly receptive state in which any input they were exposed to would be unconsciously 'absorbed'.

Despite being dismissed by mainstream learning theorists, the basic philosophy of Suggestopedia has persisted under different guises, such as *super learning, accelerated learning* and *multi-level learning*. It also prefigured a number of 'new age' learning theories that are based on questionable claims about neurobiology, such as *neurolinguistic programming* (NLP) and the belief that learners can be classified according to whether they have a visual, auditory or kinaesthetic learning style. And the quest for new ways of accelerating learning has embraced such digital technologies as augmented reality, which, allegedly, provides 'a multi-channel, high-immersion learning experience that teaches new concepts to children or adults at many times the speed and efficiency of today's standard teaching approaches' (Adams 2004).

How does it work?

The classic methodology, as pioneered by Lozanov, involves intensive classes of around four hours a day, six days a week, consisting of a dozen students who are given new, target language names and biographies. They are seated in comfortable chairs in a softly-lit, tastefully decorated room. Lessons begin with a review of the previous lesson, using standard oral practice techniques, including some kind of role play involving the spontaneous use of language. The next stage comprises the presentation and explanation of new material which takes the form of an extended written scenario with its accompanying L1 translation. The third stage is the one which most distinguishes Suggestopedia from other methods. It is called the *séance,* and aims to facilitate unconscious memorization of the new material. There are elaborate prescriptions as to how this must be done. Essentially, though, having relaxed themselves doing breathing and other exercises, the learners listen to the text – and its translation – recited aloud to them by the teacher, to the accompaniment of baroque music, whose soothing hypnotic rhythms, along with that of the teacher's carefully modulated voice, supposedly ensure maximum retention.

Does it work?

Suggestopedia aims to tap into unconscious learning faculties. Lozanov claims that material that is at the very edge of our attention and that is picked up and stored in long-term memory is actually more durable than that which is consciously learned. There is still a great deal of debate as to whether, or the extent to which, unconscious processes are implicated in SLA. On the one hand, there are those who argue that all learning requires a degree of conscious attention to what is being learned: you cannot learn in your sleep, nor when your mind is elsewhere. Others are less convinced, arguing that first language acquisition, for example, is largely an unconscious process. Thus, for Stephen Krashen (1987), an advocate of implicit – i.e. unconscious – learning, 'Suggestopedia comes very close to completely matching the requirements of optimal input' – input being the single necessary condition (especially in a stress-free environment) without which acquisition cannot occur.

To support this view, recent developments in neuroimaging suggest that explicit knowledge and implicit knowledge are differently located in the brain, and that, in an input-rich, naturalistic context, implicit – i.e. unconscious – cognitive processes are activated first – processes that appear to be the same as those operating for first language acquisition. It is plausible, then, that the kind of language exposure that Suggestopedic techniques provide, involving optimal input and low anxiety, may well activate and nourish unconscious language acquisition processes, even in adults. Whether all the 'theatre' involved in providing these conditions is necessary is, however, debatable. It may, of course, be the case that – because the students *think* that the theatre matters – it does matter, and that their learning is enhanced because of it. The method is, for all intents and purposes, a *placebo* – with all the appearances of being an effective, scientifically-grounded system, but with very little real substance. This, at least, is Earl Stevick's (1980) assessment: 'Virtually every element in a Suggestopedic course has, in addition to its overt effect, also a "placebo" effect'.

What's in it for us?

Suggestopedia – for all its pseudo-scientific and theatrical trappings – does at least attempt to address one of the single biggest challenges in language learning: the memory load. For example, current estimates of the number of word families (where a word family is a word and its common derivatives) that learners need to know in order to provide sufficient coverage for fluent reading (estimated as being 98% of the running words in a text) is anywhere from 7,000 to 9,000 words (Nation & Gu 2007). Obviously, this enormous task cannot be accomplished in the classroom alone: learners will need to read and listen to large amounts of comprehensible text in their own time, relying to some extent on incidental learning processes in order to increase their sight vocabulary. Suggestopedia's use of repeated exposure to dual-language texts offers one way that this might be accomplished.

Adams, M. (2004) *The Top Ten Technologies: #10 Superlearning Systems*. http://www.naturalnews.com/001340_learning_child_brain.html

Hansen, G.H. (1998) Lozanov and the teaching text. In Tomlinson, B. (ed.) *Materials Development in Language Teaching*. Cambridge: Cambridge University Press.

Krashen, S.D. (1987) *Principles and Practice in Second Language Acquisition*. Hemel Hempstead: Prentice Hall.

Nation, P., & Gu, P.Y. (2007) *Focus on Vocabulary*. Sydney, NSW: Macquarie University.

Stevick, E.W. (1980) *Teaching Languages: A Way and Ways*. Rowley, Mass.: Newbury House.

The Silent Way

23

When observing classes, Caleb Gattegno, founder of the Silent Way, is alleged, on occasions, to have held up a sign which simply read 'Stop teaching!'. This story captures Gattegno's fierce commitment to minimizing teachers' interventions in order to maximise the learner's own cognitive and emotional investment in the learning process. The 'silence' of the Silent Way, is the teacher's silence, not the learner's.

The background

Gattegno (1911–1988) was not, primarily, a language educator: his initial interest was in re-thinking the teaching of mathematics, especially through the use of Cuisenaire rods (small coloured blocks of wood of ten different lengths). But the guiding principle of his approach, that learners should take responsibility for, and control of, their own learning, could (he intuited) apply equally to the learning of a second language.

Basic to Gattegno's philosophy was the conviction that learning is – initially, at least – a deliberate, conscious and cognitive process, based – not on memorization or habit-formation – but on 'acts of awareness'. It follows that – for adult learners at least – the learning of a second language should in no way try to replicate the unconscious, naturalistic experience of learning the mother tongue. Gattegno aimed, instead, 'to replace a "natural" approach by one that is very "artificial" and, for some purposes, strictly controlled' (1983). Indeed, superficially at least, there is hardly a language teaching method that seems quite so artificial and controlled: unlike, say **Suggestopedia** (see chapter **22**), which at least conforms to certain folk theories of language learning, the Silent Way seems totally counter-intuitive.

Nevertheless, there are several features of the Silent Way that seem to have been imported from the **Direct Method** (see chapter **3**) and other 'natural' approaches, including the exclusive use of the target language, the symbolic use of aids to illustrate and elicit language items (i.e. the rods, as well as the colour-coded wallcharts – see below), and the strict rationing of the content to be learned, particularly vocabulary. The defining difference is, of course, the almost complete absence of teacher talk, including the question-answer sequences and corrective feedback so typical of most teaching. This 'abdication' of the teacher's traditional role is entirely in the interests of encouraging – even forcing – the learners to 'do the learning' for themselves; 'there are means of letting the learners learn while the teacher stops interfering or side-tracking' (op. cit.). Gattegno argued that the mental alertness and concentration that is required when learners are thrown back on their own resources ensures retention of the lesson content without the need for memorization: 'memory is a function of concentration' (op. cit.).

Like the other luminaries of the so-called humanistic methods movement with whom he is typically associated – Curran of **Community language learning** (see chapter **21**), and Lozanov of **Suggestopedia** (see chapter **22**) – Gattegno's rhetoric verges on the quasi-mystical at times. He invokes, for example, the 'spirit' of the language, which is encoded in its melody and rhythm and also in the difficult-to-translate small words, such as prepositions, articles and auxiliary verbs. To capture the spirit, he recommends having learners listen to recordings of authentic speech, even if they don't understand them. But underlying his thinking is a strong seam of common sense: in fact, he wrote a book called *The Common Sense of Teaching Foreign Languages*. Gattegno himself provides detailed descriptions of typical lesson sequences, while at the same time acknowledging that every learning situation and every language is different. Moreover, no two learners will follow the same learning trajectory. The teacher, therefore, should be prepared to adapt the approach to suit the local conditions and in accordance to what actually happens in the class. Nevertheless, the fundamental principle – that teaching is subordinated to learning – should dictate every decision.

How does it work?

Groups are necessarily small: all students need to be able to see and handle the set of Cuisenaire rods that the teacher manipulates. Also, the relative intimacy of the group ensures a degree of focused attention that is absolutely necessary for the kind of mental discipline that the lessons require.

Using minimal vocabulary (*rod; black, red, yellow*, etc.; *give, put, me, him, her,* etc.) and guided by colour-coded charts that display the phonemes of the language, learners construct increasingly more complex utterances in response to cues provided by the teacher. New vocabulary items or constructions may be modelled initially, but thereafter there is little or no repetition on the part of the teacher nor anything but the most minimal feedback. Instead, learners are expected to develop their own 'inner criteria' for evaluating the accuracy of their utterances. Long silences are tolerated as learners engage cognitively with the materials, trying to work out their hidden laws. As the need for more complex grammatical patterns arises, the rods are used to create contexts for these. Theoretically, at least, the entirety of a language's grammar can be built up using these minimal means.

Does it work?

For obvious reasons, the Silent Way is not widely practised, and therefore any claims as to its effectiveness are largely anecdotal. It is a procedure that is probably more often demonstrated at beginner level, as part of teaching preparation courses, than actually implemented in real classrooms with real students. Nevertheless, assuming a degree of student compliance, it's not hard to imagine it having a certain impact, in line, perhaps, with the so-called Hawthorne effect, i.e. when learners know that they are being experimented on, they tend to outperform their present competence. John Holt makes a similar point (1982):

> Perhaps this is a reason why people like Gattegno, who go around teaching demonstration maths classes, get such spectacular results. The kids know that this is not real school, that the strange man is not a teacher, that if they make mistakes nothing serious will happen, and that, in any case, it will be over soon. Thus freed from worrying, they are ready to use their brains. But how can we run a class from day to day and keep that spirit? Can it be done at all?

What's in it for us?

A method that is provocatively named the Silent Way compels us to re-evaluate the role of silence in the classroom – not as a sign of communicative failure or learner ignorance, but as a possible indicator of the cognitive effort involved in learning. As Claire Kramsch (2009) argues:

> We may want to leave time in class for students to write in silence, to have a silent, private contact with the shape of a poem and its silent sounds, to listen in silence to the cadences of a student or to our own voice reading aloud, to follow silently the rhythm of a conversation played on tape, the episodic structure of a story well told. We may want to even foster silence as a way of letting the students reflect on what they are right now experiencing.

Moreover, Gattegno's guiding principle – that teachers should intervene less so that learners develop their own autonomous learning skills – is a basic tenet of any approach that subscribes to the notion of learner-centeredness. Although Gattegno pushed this principle to the limits of credibility, many – maybe most – teachers might be well advised, from time to time, to follow Gattegno's injunction to simply 'stop teaching'.

Gattegno, C. (1983) The silent way. In Oller, J.W., Richard-Amato, P.A. (eds) *Methods that Work: A Smorgasbord of Ideas for Language Teachers.* Rowley, Mass.: Newbury House.

Holt, J. (1982) *How Children Fail (Revised Edition).* Cambridge, Mass: Da Capo Press.

Kramsch, C. (2009) *The Multilingual Subject.* Oxford: Oxford University Press.

Crazy English & the Rassias method

24

'In order to be a wit in a foreign language you have to go through the stage of being a half-wit,' wrote Peter Harder in 1985. These two methods take this premise to its logical conclusion.

The background

Li Yang (born 1969) was a student of mechanical engineering in Lanzhou University, China. Pathologically shy, his grades were poor, especially in English, which he needed in order to graduate. Driven to desperate measures, he discovered that the recitation of his English texts as preparation for his exams was much more effective if he went outside and – rather than mumbling the sentences to himself – simply shouted them at the top of his voice. He passed his English exam with flying colours. Encouraged by this unexpected breakthrough, he started teaching English on the side. A brief stint as an English presenter on television led to his setting up, in 1994, a teaching and publishing venture called Crazy English, which he energetically publicised by giving lessons to large groups in public venues. By 1997 Li Yang was a celebrity, filling whole sports stadiums with English language learners chanting in unison. Astute merchandising of CDs, DVDs and books (including his autobiography *I am Crazy, I Succeed*) helped spread his method further: his followers numbering in the tens of millions, allegedly.

Li Yang is not the only, or even the first, 'crazy' teacher. When John Rassias (1925–2015), the son of Greek immigrants to the USA, started teaching French – the subject he had majored in – there was little in the method or the materials that enthused him. It was only when he realized that his other great love – the theatre – could be enlisted into the teaching of languages that he began to formulate what became known as the Rassias Method. He pioneered the method teaching Peace Corps volunteers as preparation for postings to French-speaking Africa in the 1960s, and further refined it in Dartmouth, Vermont, where he trained hundreds of teachers in its techniques. Essentially, these include rapid-fire drilling coupled with comically exaggerated feedback, as well as role playing and the acting out of 'skits'. What both Li Yang and Rassias have in common is a repertoire of performance skills by means of which they make fairly conventional techniques – such as drilling – non-threatening, highly entertaining, and hence (they would both claim) extremely memorable.

How does it work?

Both Crazy English and the Rassias method borrow from **audiolingualism** (see chapter 6), and incorporate intensive drilling of structural patterns – so intensive, in the case of Rassias, that the drilling is usually conducted by adjuncts, while the teacher's role is reserved for the less regimented, more performance-based stages of each lesson. The purpose of the drilling, for Rassias, seems to be less about habituation than about maximising student talking time: each student is expected to speak at least 65 times in the course of a 50-minute lesson. This also accounts for the rapid delivery of question-and-answer routines, in which teachers are encouraged to snap their fingers to keep things moving. Feedback on accuracy is provided by exaggerated gestures, such as blowing kisses (in the case of a correct answer) or miming a knife thrust (in the case of error). On the other hand, accuracy is not necessarily the main goal. As Rassias is quoted as saying (Wolkomir 1983), 'Have the courage to be bad, to make mistakes – but speak!'.

In Crazy English, drilling is done mainly for the purposes of confidence building and for memorization, and in that sense it fits into a well-established Chinese tradition of recitation and repetition. Videos of Li Yang show him drilling huge crowds in utterances like 'Would you like to speak English?', a word at a time until the whole utterance is shouted in its entirety. This is part of what he calls 'tongue muscle training'. Students are also taught to mimic 20 different gestures representing different English phonemes. Compared to the Rassias method, Crazy English is much less intensive, especially when conducted as a self-study program: in the interests of avoiding overload and the associated loss of confidence, the sentences to be learned are delivered in manageable sets – e.g. ten a month – and a prize is awarded once each set is 'learned'.

Does it work?

Both Rassias and Li Yang seem less preoccupied with the mechanics of teaching and much more focused on removing the inhibitions that block language learning, whatever method is employed. The website for Dartmouth College (where Rassias developed his program) states:

> The goal of the Rassias Method is to make the participant feel comfortable and natural with the language in a short period of time. This is accomplished through a specific series of teaching procedures and dramatic techniques which seek to eliminate inhibitions and create an atmosphere of free expression from the very first day of class.

Similarly, Li Yang's personal struggle to overcome his fear of 'losing face' is a theme he returns to frequently, as justification for the 'craziness' of his approach. For example, he has his students chant 'I'm not afraid of losing face!'. In fact, his approach seems to target not just language learning but personal self-esteem and, ultimately, self-realization: he is quoted as saying 'You have to make a lot of mistakes. You have to be laughed at by a lot of people. But that doesn't matter, because your future is totally different from other people's futures' (Osnos 2008).

Judged in these terms, then, the enthusiasm with which both methods have been received would seem to confirm that, in terms of breaking down inhibitions, they do succeed. Rassias's long association with the Peace Corps, for example, suggests his initial courses provide an effective platform for subsequent immersive learning while in the field. And the rapturous, almost cult-like, response that Li Yang evokes must have impelled at least some of his many fans into dedicating more time and effort into learning English.

On the negative side, it may be that, for certain learners at least, the mindless chanting, the play-acting and, above all, the assertive presence of their larger-than-life teachers are a disincentive. For every student who reports that 'having an egg broken over your head by Rassias is an intense loving experience' (Wolkomir 1983), there will be at least one who will likely be less well disposed.

What's in it for us?

To paraphrase the old workplace slogan: *You don't have to be crazy to teach here, but it helps.* In other words, any method, however discredited, can be made to work if the teacher injects a degree of novelty, theatricality and surprise. More importantly, any techniques that serve to reduce the learners' fears and insecurities – whether or not these techniques are as extreme as either Li Yang's or Rassias's – will go at least some way to ensuring a method's chances of success.

Harder, P. (1980). Discourse and self-expression – on the reduced personality of the second language learner. *Applied Linguistics*, 1: 262–270.

Osnos, E. (2008) Crazy English: The national scramble to learn a new language before the Olympics. *The New Yorker*, April 28. http://www.newyorker.com/magazine/2008/04/28/crazy-english (accessed 17th January 2017)

Rassias Centre, Dartmouth College: http://rassias.dartmouth.edu/method/

Wolkomir, R. (1983) A manic professor tries to close up the language gap. In Oller, J.W., Richard-Amato, P.A. (eds) *Methods that Work: A Smorgasbord of Ideas for Language Teachers*. Rowley, Mass.: Newbury House.

E: Self-study methods

Over time, self-study methods have adapted to changes in technology (from the printed book to long-playing records to mobile phones) while tending to reflect – rather than lead – contemporary developments in classroom methodology. But there have been some notable innovations, some of which are reviewed in this section.

> Before there were linguists there were 'philologists' –
> literally, 'lovers of learning'. One of the most famous,
> William 'Oriental' Jones (1746–1794), reputedly knew
> 28 languages.

Background

Interest in so-called 'oriental' languages by Western scholars in the
18th and 19th centuries was fuelled by – among other things – a
burgeoning interest in archaeology and in 'philology', or what now
would be known as comparative linguistics. This produced a cadre of
Western 'orientalists', many of whom, because formal instruction in the
languages they wanted to learn was often not available, were self-taught
polyglots. The methods they used are still of interest, not least for what
they tell us about learner autonomy and agency. In this section we will
look at just two of these 19th century orientalists: Sir Richard Burton
(1821–1890), the British explorer, spy, diplomat, and translator of the
Arabian Nights, who was allegedly fluent in 29 languages, and Ármin
Vámbéry (1832–1913), the Hungarian 'turkologist' (and also a spy),
who used his knowledge of Turkish to argue the case for a common
origin between that language and Hungarian.

How did it work?

Both Burton and Vámbéry have left accounts of their methods, the
former being more detailed than the latter, but both coinciding in their
reliance on memorization, reading aloud, and the use of authentic texts.

Here is Burton (1893, quoted in Brodie 1967/1986):

> I got a simple grammar and vocabulary, marked out the forms and
> words which I knew were absolutely necessary, and learnt them by
> heart by carrying them in my pocket and looking over them at spare
> moments during the day. I never worked for more than a quarter of an
> hour at a time, for after that the brain lost its freshness. After learning

some three hundred words, easily done in a week, I stumbled through some easy book-work (one of the Gospels is the most come-atable), and underlined every word that I wished to recollect, in order to read over my pencillings at least once a day … If I came across a new sound like the Arabic *Ghayn*, I trained my tongue to it by repeating it so many thousand times a day. When I read, I invariably read out loud, so that the ear might aid memory … Whenever I conversed with anybody in a language I was learning, I took the trouble to repeat their words inaudibly after them, and so to learn the trick of pronunciation and emphasis.

Burton's text-based approach closely matches that of his German contemporary, the archaeologist Heinrich Schliemann (quoted in Lomb 1988/2013):

In order to acquire quickly the Greek vocabulary, I procured a modern Greek translation of *Paul et Virginie*, and read it through, comparing every word with its equivalent in the French original. When I had finished this task I knew at least one half the Greek words the book contained; and after repeating the operation I knew them all, or nearly so, without having lost a single minute by being obliged to use a dictionary […] Of the Greek grammar I learned only the declensions and the verbs, and never lost my precious time in studying its rules.

Meanwhile, Vámbéry, who had grown up bilingual in Hungarian and German, polylingualism was early acquired. He recalls (1889) that 'I found myself, not quite sixteen years old, conversant with so many principal languages that acquiring the idioms [i.e. dialects] kindred to them had become a comparatively easy task for me'. Here he recounts his approach:

I always took special delight in memorizing. … When I was able to increase the number of words which I could master in one day from ten to sixty and even to a hundred, my exultation knew no bounds. … I never omitted to read out loud and to hold conversations with myself in the languages I was learning … .

Having gained a basic grasp of the language he was learning, he moved on to 'general literature' which he read aloud, often gesturing as he did so. ('Owing to this habit of loud reading and the violent gestures with which I would often accompany it, the plain people who were about me often thought me wrong in the mind.') If available, he would consult a translation of the text he was reading (he admits he was too poor to afford a dictionary), and he annotated the texts with his feelings 'whenever any passage happened to strike my imagination'.

Did it work?

While there is no independent evidence as to the degree of proficiency achieved by either Burton or Vámbéry, we do know that Burton's fluency in Arabic, Persian and Hindustani enabled him to 'pass' as a Muslim (of Pathan origins but resident in Rangoon) and visit the otherwise off-limits holy sites of Medina and Mecca.

As for Vámbéry, it was on his first journey abroad, en route from Budapest to Istanbul, that he was given an opportunity to put his theoretical knowledge of Serbian, Italian, and Turkish to practice with his fellow shipboard passengers. He immediately became the centre of attention: 'They formed a ring around me, trying to guess at my nationality, and received rather sceptically my statement that I had never been abroad'. And he adds that, after only a day or two, he had improved his Turkish to such an extent that, on arriving in Turkey, he was able to act as a Turkish interpreter for a fellow Hungarian.

What's in it for us?

It is difficult to generalise on the basis of these two cases, but what is interesting is the way that the two orientalists used the (solitary) academic study of the systems of the target language as a launching pad into actual use of the language as meaningful communication. Contradicting the immersionist view, i.e. that you learn a language by using it, there was a clear distinction between the learning and using phases in both Burton's and Vámbéry's cases. This is consistent with the nineteenth century view of learning as being an intellectual, rather than an experiential, endeavour. As Henry Sweet (1899/1964) argued, 'It sounds well to talk of "picking up a language by ear in the country itself", but most good linguists will confess that they learnt nearly everything from books, and but little from conversation'. There is a body of research that would seem to vindicate the view that, at least for some learners and in some learning contexts (typically instructed ones), the learning of the facts of the language, e.g. its grammar rules, reinforced by cycles of practice, is as effective, if not more so, than more 'deep-end' approaches. Subscribing to a view of learning that is known as 'skills acquisition theory', these studies suggest that *declarative knowledge* (i.e. facts) can become *proceduralized* (i.e. turned into skilled behaviours) through practice. What is unusual, perhaps, in the case of both Burton and Vámbéry, is that the practice activities included reading aloud, an activity that is nowadays generally discouraged by advocates of more communicative approaches.

Brodie, F.M. (1967/1986) *The Devil Drives: A Life of Sir Richard Burton*. London: Eland.

Lomb, K. (1988/2013) *Harmony of Babel: Profiles of Famous Polyglots of Europe*. Translated by S. Alkire. Berkeley: TESL-EJ Publications.

Vámbéry, A. (1889) *Árminius Vámbéry, His Life and Adventures*. London: Fisher Unwin.

Prendergast's 'Mastery System'

Thomas Prendergast (1806–1886) was another nineteenth century 'orientalist' (see chapter 24). But, unlike his peers, who were content simply to boast about their linguistic prowess, Prendergast attempted to turn his own language learning experience into a method that could be generalized to other languages and for other learners.

Background

Like his father before him, Prendergast served all his working life in the East India Company, during which time he learned at least two of India's indigenous languages, Hindustani and Telugu. On retirement in his fifties, he returned to England where (now blind) he spent his remaining years developing what he called his 'Mastery' system, published in 1864 as *The Mastery of Languages or, the Art of Speaking Foreign Tongues Idiomatically*, along with accompanying teaching materials in a variety of languages. Based largely on his own experience as a learner, (he never actually taught languages himself), his method was directed at self-study rather than classroom instruction (although he did provide guidance for teachers, just in case).

Essentially, his method involved the cumulative memorization of a set of exemplary sentences and the subset of sentences that can be derived (or 'evolved') from each of them. Unlike other approaches within the then current **Grammar-Translation** (see chapter 10) paradigm, Prendergast's sentences were not graded from the simple to the more complex. Rather, they were deliberately contrived to pack in as much syntax as possible, the test of their usefulness being the number of less complex sentences that could be generated from them. Supposedly, this replicated the 'natural' process by which children pick up a second language: somehow they are able to extract an entire grammar out of the 'chance' sentences that they are exposed to, and without these being graded in any significant way. How do they do this? With remarkable foresight, Prendergast had observed that children seem to achieve fluency by memorizing entire sequences of words – what we would now call chunks or constructions. They are also able to combine and re-combine these elements in creative ways. Accordingly, Prendergast set about trying to identify the most frequent constructions, albeit only those that qualified as well-formed sentences. Because children are able to derive the grammar from these constructions without explicit instruction, Prendergast was adamant that all grammar explanation was 'prohibited', not only because it interfered with natural processes, but because it was redundant. As he argued, 'When a man has committed to memory a few well selected sentences, each containing different constructions, and has acquired the power of putting them together in all their variations, one rapid perusal of the grammar will suffice to convince him that he is already in possession of the whole syntax of the language' (1864).

Moreover, the vocabulary load was to be kept light – partly so as to reduce the demands on memory (since 'the capacity of the memory for the retention of foreign words is universally over-estimated'), but also because he believed that a core vocabulary was sufficient to encapsulate the essential features of the language being studied. As he wrote (1864), 'When a child can employ two hundred words of a foreign language he possesses a practical knowledge of all the syntactical constructions and of all the foreign sounds'. Accordingly, Prendergast compiled a list of the 200 or so most frequent words in English and, although he obviously had no access to digitalized corpora, his intuitions were impressively accurate.

How did it work?

The learner studying alone first memorizes one of the target sentences, for which there is a translation. For example, the first sentence in the French course is:

> *Pourquois ne voulez-vous pas me faire le plaisir de passer demain avec moi chez le frère de notre ami dans la rue Neuve?* (Why will you not do me the favour of calling on our friend's brother in New Street with me tomorrow?)

'Variations' of this sentence are then supplied, e.g. *Voulez-vous me faire le plaisir? Voulez-vous le faire? Vous ne voulez pas me faire le plaisir. Voulez-vous le faire?* etc. These are to be memorized and their recall tested by translating from their English versions (supplied on each facing page) into French. Once one sentence and its variations have been thoroughly learned – to the extent that they can be recalled flawlessly and at speed – the learner moves to the next sentence: in the French course, this translates as *Do you not want to go to London today, before your morning walk, to have your boots stretched at the French shoemaker's?* (Authenticity was clearly not a priority for Prendergast!) And so on, for another 13 sentences and over a thousand variations.

Does it work?

Prendergast's Mastery System seems to have enjoyed some degree of success in its time and was adapted to the teaching of four other languages as well as French, all of which ran to several editions. It was also adopted by other writers in the design of their own courses. But it was soon overtaken by less cerebral approaches to language learning, notably the **Direct Method** (see chapter 3).

Nevertheless, in many ways, Prendergast's system prefigured developments in methodology that were way ahead of their time. One of these was the use of what later came to be known as *substitution tables*: i.e. tables that display the way that words and sentence elements can be combined. Also, his belief that mastery of a limited 'core' of structures and vocabulary could serve as a foundation for later proficiency contrasted with his contemporaries, for whom principles of selection or grading were largely ignored. But perhaps most remarkable was his insight that fluency, at least in part, results from having a memorized store of fixed and semi-fixed formulaic utterances – 'Language is a tree which is propagated not by seeds, but by cuttings' (1864) – even if he misunderstood the nature of these 'cuttings' – i.e. that they typically consist, not of complete sentences, but of phrases. Nor was it entirely clear how learners were to transition from memorizing the pre-selected variations to creating original, meaningful utterances of their own. Moreover, the reliance on sentences rather than connected text, and extremely contrived sentences at that, meant that

Prendergast's system was unfairly lumped together with those of his grammar-translation contemporaries.

What's in it for us?

As a self-study method, though, the Mastery System had one saving strength – a recognition of the value of what we now call *distributed practice*, i.e. short bursts of practice distributed over increasingly longer intervals. As Prendergast put it, 'in learning anything by heart, repetitions are indispensable, and the more they are distributed throughout the day, the smaller will be the number required to impress the foreign phrases on the memory' (1870). To expedite this, Prendergast recommended that learners carry around with them both the L1 and L2 sentences, and, after first reading the latter, they should attempt to translate the L1 sentences into the L2, unseen. Moreover, this should be done in 'irregular succession', i.e. in a different order each time.

These same principles underpin the use of vocabulary learning 'word cards', whereby learners review vocabulary by translating into and out of their L1. The principle has now been successfully digitalized and refined, and downloadable apps, with which learners can input their own word (or phrase) lists and regularly review them in randomized order, are freely available and massively popular. Prendergast would have approved.

Prendergast, T. (1864) *The Mastery of Languages, or the Art of Speaking Foreign Tongues Idiomatically*. London: R. Bentley.

Prendergast, T. (1870) *The Mastery Series: French (New Edition)*. New York: Appleton & Co.

27 Brand name Methods: Assimil, Michel Thomas, Pimsleur

> Methods that were branded with the name of their inventor were common in the nineteenth century, the Ollendorf Method and the Berlitz Method being but two. The tradition persists.

Background

'My tailor is rich'. The first example sentence of *Anglais sans peine* ('English without toil' 1929), in turn the first publication of the Assimil group, has iconic status – encapsulating as it does the distinctive style of self-study manuals, instantly recognizable to generations of long-suffering autodidacts. Its author, Alphonse Chérel (1882–1956), was himself an autodidact, having left his native France to work as a private teacher in Tsarist Russia, where he learned Russian. Thence he moved to England and then Germany, where he picked up English and German respectively. At the time, virtually the only way to learn a foreign language, apart from living in the country where the language was spoken, was to attend a Berlitz-type school or get a private teacher. Aged 46, Chérel decided to remedy the situation by producing a calendar, on every page of which there was a short, light-hearted English lesson for self-study. From this seed the mighty Assimil empire was born, and it flourishes to this day.

Michel Thomas (1914–2005) was similarly motivated to exploit his polyglot achievements, although his life was considerably more colourful than Chérel's. Born in Poland, he moved to France to escape the Nazis, and then (allegedly) joined the French resistance, before working as a spy for the US. He was frequently arrested and tortured but attributed his survival, on more than one occasion, to his linguistic skills. After the war he emigrated to California, where he set up a language school in 1947. His distinctive teaching style and extravagant claims (e.g. that conversational proficiency could be achieved after just three intensive days' instruction) soon attracted the attention of, among

110 | *Scott Thornbury's 30 Language Teaching Methods*

others, the great and good of Hollywood, including Grace Kelly, Woody Allen and Emma Thompson. He started merchandising his approach as a self-study course, and it is still widely marketed as the Michel Thomas Method.

Unlike either Chérel or Thomas, Paul Pimsleur (1927–1976), had a strong academic background, including a PhD in French, which he taught in California, before taking up a position at Ohio State University. There he set up the Listening Center, one of the largest language laboratories in the U.S., where he experimented with self-paced language teaching programmes designed according to the prevailing audiolingual methodology. Invited to Washington D.C. in 1962 to advise on how foreign language teaching in the U.S. could be improved, Pimsleur 'proposed creating a self-study audio language programme based on his own classroom methodology and his experience with students at the Listening Center' (Pimsleur 1980/2013). The first course – for learning Greek – was launched in 1963; now owned and marketed by Simon & Schuster, the Pimsleur catalogue offers self-study courses in over 50 different languages.

How do they work?

All three methods borrow from – and perpetuate – features of the methods that were dominant at their time of creation. But, in different ways, they each incorporate elements that are designed to meet the challenge of teacher-less instruction. Pre-dating Communicative Language Teaching, the syllabuses of all three are predominantly structural, although explicit grammar instruction is kept to a minimum: grammar, it is assumed, will be acquired inductively simply through exposure to, and repetition of, example sentences. In the case of Michel Thomas, syntax is built up incrementally though the combination of words (initially often cognates) and phrases. The vocabulary input in all three courses is deliberately restricted, presumably so as to avoid overload.

Texts, if they exist at all, are typically scripted dialogues. To ensure understanding, the input in all three courses is translated into the learner's L1, and explanations and instructions are also provided in the L1. Both Michel Thomas and the Pimsleur courses are purely spoken – there is no written support. The Assimil courses, by contrast, have an accompanying coursebook, each double-page spread divided between the L2 and the L1 translation. They also have a curious division into receptive and productive phases: for the first half of the 100-unit course, learners simply listen and read. Half-way through they return to the beginning and this time translate the texts and example sentences of each unit from their L1 into the target language.

In all three courses, interaction occurs mainly in the form of repeating sentences on the recordings. In Pimsleur, the response time is carefully calibrated so as to optimise the principle of spaced repetition, i.e. successive responses are required at increasingly longer intervals. The original Michel Thomas course is unique in that Thomas himself is present on the audio recordings: he is heard conducting each lesson with two students, pausing at points to elicit responses from the user.

Do they work?

Given the decades of uninterrupted sales these courses have enjoyed, it might seem perverse to even question their effectiveness. They must be working for somebody. Certainly, in his time Michel Thomas attracted an almost cult-like following in Hollywood: Emma Thompson is on record as saying that her crash course in Spanish was 'the most extraordinary learning experience of my life – it was unforgettable'. Of course, that was a one-to-one course, not the self-study version. In fact, given the lack of real interaction or point-of-need feedback in the self-study courses, it's hard to credit the claims made in the publicity for these courses, each purporting to cut learning time radically, and promising the learner enviable levels of fluency for just 30 minutes' study a day. Because the only feedback the learner gets is on their ability to recall by heart the artificially limited input and not on their capacity to engage in real communication, it may be that learners are under the illusion that they are progressing, even if they are not. At best, these courses might provide a foundation on which to build in subsequent immersive situations. Users of this and similar methods attest to the confidence that is instilled as, through regular re-playing of the recorded material, they become 'acclimatized' to what was initially just meaningless noise. Likewise, the initial memorization, through repeated practice, of key words and phrases provides a foothold into an otherwise impenetrable system.

What's in it for us?

The need for self-study courses is as acute as ever; the technological means for satisfying this need have increased exponentially since the first Assimil course was published. Many of the shortcomings of these courses – such as the lack of opportunities for real time interaction – could relatively easily be remedied by signing up for some sort of language exchange, such as that offered by Conversation Exchange (www.conversationexchange.com). Moreover, most language learning apps (see chapter **28 Programmed Instruction: Duolingo**) now include a social networking component that allows 'real' interaction. Likewise, vocabulary learning apps can be used to boost the lexical input, while the internet, in conjunction with translation software, provides a much richer diet of authentic texts than any of these courses presently offer.

Pimsleur, P. (1980/2013) *How to Learn a Foreign Language*. New York: Pimsleur Language Programs.

28 Programmed Instruction: Duolingo

> Digital technologies 'atomize educational processes and practices into a series of discrete tasks' (Selwyn 2014). Even before the advent of digital technologies, the 'atomization' of language teaching was well underway.

The background

The name B.F. Skinner (1904–1990) is inextricably linked to behaviourist learning theory. This is the theory that learning is an effect of behaviour change, and that behaviours can be changed by reinforcing the preferred response to a stimulus through the provision of positive or negative feedback. Even before the advent of the computer chip, Skinner was quick to realize that these behaviourist principles could be executed by mechanical means. Accordingly, he set about designing machine-readable programmes that segmented the learning material into small steps, where progress from one step to the next depended on a correct response to each successive task. Not only that, the teaching machines were, ideally at least, 'adaptive', in the sense that the choice of each step was contingent on how the learner answered the preceding one, requiring a 'branching' rather than a 'linear' program. It is only through branching, argues Valdman (1966) that the ultimate goals of computer-based programs can be realised: 'complete control of the learner's behaviour, involving immediate and reliable feedback and adaptation to individual learning habits at each step of the way'.

By these means, learners could (theoretically, at least) work at their own pace and in accordance to their own learning needs. Of course, to anticipate all the possible 'branches' that even one individual learner might generate was a computational task way beyond the scope of programmers in Skinner's day (and, arguably, of programmers even now). Nevertheless, the basic principles of 'programmed instruction' had been established, and all that was needed was to apply them to language teaching.

This was already being done, in a variety of languages, by the early 1950s under the name of Audio-Lingual Language Programming. But, by the 1970s, with the demise of **audiolingualism** (see chapter 6), programmed instruction – never hugely popular at the best of times – had completely fallen out of favour. It wasn't until the widespread use of mobile devices, plus an exponential increase in computing power, that programmed instruction was rehabilitated and delivered by means of language learning apps.

One of the first of these apps to achieve global success was Duolingo, launched in 2012 by co-founders Luis von Ahn and Severin Hacker, with the express aim of providing a language learning tool that was free, fun to use, and effective. As in the original programmed instruction machines, users are led from one challenge to the next. But – despite the branching possibilities offered by digital software – the learning path is essentially linear. In order to short-cut any stages in the lesson sequence, a user can 'test out', but this is one of the very few concessions to 'personalization'.

And, true to the Skinnerian principle of positive reinforcement, Duolingo includes an element of 'gamification', i.e. design features borrowed from computer games. Thus, Duolingo users are rewarded (in the form of 'lingots') for achieving their daily targets, and are encouraged to compete with friends, workmates, or other learners in the 'Duolingo Clubs'.

To date Duolingo offers around 80 different courses (e.g. English for Spanish speakers; French for German speakers etc.), and boasts millions of registered users (although how many are regularly active users is unknown). And – thanks to the hosting of ads – it is free, although a fee-paying testing service has also been launched for some languages.

How does it work?

On signing in, users are presented with their learning 'roadmap' and are prompted to set their own learning goals, in terms of the amount of time they plan to study daily, and the number of points they hope to gain (but not of *what* they would like to learn – there are only limited options in terms of what they can choose to focus on within their present level).

By means of multiple matching tasks (e.g. of words with pictures), reading aloud tasks (evaluated by voice recognition software), and the translating of short sentences, they are led through a series of tasks that are organised into a gamified 'skill tree' that targets the learning of a specific grammatical structure or a lexical set. As the website says, 'language is split into bite-size skills that feel like games' (Duolingo). Meaning is conveyed by translation, or, in the case of vocabulary, pictures, and there are no explicit grammar rules, although feedback on incorrect answers often includes a brief explanation. Learners are rewarded once they have completed all the exercises associated with the specific 'skill'. They are also presented with graphic feedback on their strengths and weaknesses, and prompted to work on the latter. In this sense, the methodology is essentially a streamlined version of programmed learning, the difference being that sophisticated algorithms recycle the learning content at intervals that are calibrated to maximise memorization, on the principle of 'spaced repetition'. But the object, as with programmed learning, is 'complete control of the learner's behaviour'.

More recently, Duolingo has incorporated a 'chatbot' feature for some languages: learners interact with the program to role-play a situation, e.g. ordering a meal in a restaurant, by keying in their responses to the pre-programmed 'waiter'. The program accepts a limited range of responses, but rejects any response that is grammatically incorrect or contextually inappropriate.

Does it work?

While Duolingo cites a research study that shows that 34 hours of Duolingo is the equivalent of one whole semester of university-level language instruction, there is little if any independent investigation into its effectiveness. Like many digital self-study tools, Duolingo has been criticised for its 'old-fashioned', somewhat mechanical approach, including its narrow focus on discrete-items of grammar, its reliance on de-contextualized sentences, and the built-in assumption that accuracy is a prerequisite for fluency. Moreover, its contrived language examples undermine any claims to be authentic or even accurate. Nor are there opportunities for creative language use, nor real (i.e. human-to-human) interaction. All this suggests that Duolingo (and similar apps) might work best to complement, rather than substitute for, 'live' learning in classrooms.

What's in it for us?

Apart from being free, what, then, explains Duolingo's phenomenal success? As well as its attractive and user-friendly interface, users invariably highlight the built-in motivation provided by the gamification software, and the sense of immediate gratification that this supplies: as the website boasts, 'it's addictive!'. They also value the element of surprise, in not quite knowing what type of exercise they will be served next, while at the same time appreciating the spaced repetition of tasks that maximises their memorability. And, of course, there is its portability and the fact that the learner can brush up whenever they have a spare moment, wherever they are.

But the real takeaway is doubtlessly the sense that learners get that they are constantly and incrementally improving – improvement that they can attribute to their own agency, given that they set their own learning targets. The system is oriented towards success at every step.

Duolingo: https://www.duolingo.com/

Selwyn, N. (2014) *Distrusting Educational Technology*. London: Routledge.

Valdmann, A. (1966) Programmed instruction and foreign language teaching. In Valdmann, A. (ed.) *Trends in Language Teaching*. New York: McGraw-Hill.

Online Polyglots

Key the word 'polyglot' into an internet search engine and you will be inundated with links to websites or videos in which individuals who have achieved success in a number of languages both demonstrate their linguistic achievements and offer advice to other, potential polyglots.

Background

Benny Lewis, for example, is a typical case: a failed classroom learner, he opted for immersion and self-instruction, using a variety of online and print sources, and now speaks 'over a dozen languages'. Like Lewis, many of the 'professional' (and predominantly male) polyglots are self-taught. Those that do attend formal classes typically reinforce classroom instruction with a great deal of extra-curricular and self-initiated practice. And, for many, formal study, whether curricular or extra-curricular, is often combined with a period spent living in a place where the language is spoken.

The experience of learning several languages has given many the confidence to recommend – if not a method as such – at least certain strategies that predict success. As a consequence, some have developed self-help guides, learning materials, and entire language courses. There are now so many of these self-taught polyglots that hundreds of them meet annually at conferences in both North America and Europe. Significantly, perhaps, few have any academic background in educational theory or in linguistics, and seldom if ever reference the literature on SLA in their blog posts. This apparent indifference is mutual: despite their often extraordinary achievements, self-taught polyglots are virtually ignored in the SLA research literature.

How does it work?

While each online polyglot has a slightly different approach to language learning, conditioned as it is by their very different life stories and learning trajectories, there are enough commonalities to constitute what could be considered a generic 'self-help' method. Based on these shared principles, this 'über-method' might best be characterized as nativist, communicatively-oriented and socially-constructed.

It is nativist in the sense that the default model of language acquisition is the child learning his or her mother tongue, i.e. a naturalistic and immersive one. As Lewis (2014), puts it, 'the way to learn a language is to live it'. Hence, there is often a blanket rejection of procedures associated with formal language learning, such as studying grammar rules, rote learning and (to a lesser extent) translation. As Donovan Nagel argues, 'you didn't become a fluent speaker of your own language by studying its grammar' (The Mezzofanti Guild). Indeed, there is a built-in assumption that most formal instruction still follows grammar-translation principles.

By contrast, today's autodidacts are communicatively oriented, and promote a 'fluency-first' approach. 'Speak from day 1' is Lewis's slogan. Or, as Anthony Lauder puts it (quoted on The Polyglot Dream website), 'fluency is not an end goal, but a springboard from which you can keep getting better and better'. This may mean sacrificing accuracy and 'embracing a little imperfection', in Lewis's words. It also means adopting a risk-taking strategy and a 'willingness to communicate'. As a foothold into fluency, many recommend memorizing some high-frequency phrases, although only a few (e.g. Nagel) acknowledge the central role of prefabricated 'chunks' in developing overall proficiency.

Most, if not all, autodidacts foreground the social function of language and the belief that acquisition is socially constructed. As Lindsay Dow argues, 'it's a common truth by now that we need human interaction to communicate well in a language'. Lewis (op. cit.) suggests that social interaction is not only necessary but sufficient:

> We keep trying to find language solutions through courses, software, apps, flights abroad, books, schools, and a host of other methods, some of which can be useful, but these are nothing but accessories to the true core of language-learning: the people we speak with and hear.

For many, this is what motivates them, i.e. contact with other people and cultures: language learning and travel are inextricably connected.

Less weight is given to the development of literacy skills, and it is generally accepted that pronunciation, while important, need not be native-like so long as it is intelligible – although some, like Gabriel Wyner (2014) would dispute this: 'An accurate accent is powerful because it is the ultimate gesture of empathy'.

Perhaps of most significance are the learning strategies that these polyglots enlist, especially for vocabulary acquisition. These include the use of word cards (or their digital equivalent), spaced repetition, a reliance on cognates (at least initially), contextualization, and mnemonic techniques, such as associating words with memorable images. Other form-focused strategies that are mentioned are: shadowing (i.e. listening to a recording and sub-vocalizing at the same time), transcribing spoken language, and reverse translation (i.e. translating a text from L2 into L1 and then back again, unseen). Unlike the promoters of Brand name methods, autodidacts acknowledge that language learning takes a good deal of time and concentrated effort: for example, Alexander Arguelles, a 'hyper-polyglot', attributes his phenomenal success to 'drive, discipline, countless hours of systematic hard work, sustained interest and motivation, access to good materials and intelligent methods and procedures for using them'.

Nevertheless, the experience of learning several languages has taught polyglots how to cut corners, and even 'fake it'. As Richard Simcott puts it, 'that doesn't mean that [we] are fakes. It simply means that [we] can get by on far less ... we learn to be fluent with what we've got'.

Does it work?

If we take them at their word, these polyglots have achieved impressive – in some cases, superhuman – feats of language learning. It has clearly worked for them, especially when combined with immersion in the target language community. What none of them mentions, however, is *aptitude*, i.e. an innate talent for language learning. Research suggests that aptitude is not evenly distributed across populations. Notwithstanding, many of these polyglots are insistent that there is no bar, including age, to achieving fluency in at least one other language. Nevertheless, their up-beat optimism and questionable claims need to be tempered with a little caution: some people are just not good language learners.

What's in it for us?

What stands out from all these accounts is these learners' *agency* – in the sense that they are the instigators and managers of their own learning. This is reflected in their choice of learning strategies: the *metacognitive*, such as the way they set realistic and achievable goals, and the way they actively seek out the best technological aids for their purposes; the *cognitive*, such as their choice of vocabulary learning techniques, or the deliberate attention given to form; and the *social*, such as setting up conversation exchanges, either on-line or face-to-face, or finding a 'buddy' to share their learning experiences with. These learners have really learned how to learn. Their combined wisdom, in the form of proven learning strategies, along with their infectious enthusiasm for language learning, is worth sharing with classroom learners.

Arguelles, A. http://www.foreignlanguageexpertise.com/

Dow, L. http://www.lindsaydoeslanguages.com/

Lewis, B. (2014) *Fluent in 3 Months: Tips and Techniques to Help You Learn Any Language.* London: HarperCollins.

The Mezzofanti Guild http://www.mezzoguild.com/

Simcott, R. http://speakingfluently.com/

The Polyglot Dream: http://www.thepolyglotdream.com

Wyner, G. (2014) *Fluent Forever: How to Learn Any Language Fast and Never Forget It.* New York: Harmony.

F: Beyond methods

Although methods were declared dead in the 1990s, the method concept still persists, even if only as a kind of *smorgasbord* from which teachers can pick and choose, tailoring their methodology to their particular context. That is to say that, even in the absence of methods, mindful teachers still go about their work 'methodically'.

---

30 Principled Eclecticism

Principled Eclecticism

> Twenty-nine methods and still counting: what are we
> to make of this steady drip-feed – sometimes a tsunami
> – of methods? Why are there so many, and how is the
> practising teacher to choose between them?

Background

One reason for the plethora of methods is that we still do not know
everything there is to know about how people learn languages – whether
their first language or an additional one. The study of second language
acquisition (SLA) is a relatively new field (as scientific fields go). While
we are much better informed than we were half a century ago, there
are still some key questions over which there is a great deal of debate.
These include:

1. To what extent is SLA like first language acquisition?
2. To what extent does SLA involve conscious vs. unconscious learning
   processes?
3. Why do learners make mistakes?
4. How do you become fluent?
5. Why do some learners do better than others?

As new research findings come to light, and new theories are
generated to explain them, old methods adapt or new methods are
invented to take account of these developments. The **Lexical Approach**
(see chapter **11**), for example, was largely influenced by insights from
the study of language corpora. And **Task-based Language Teaching**
(see chapter **16**) draws heavily on research into cognition. On the
other hand, research seldom yields findings that are 100 percent
conclusive. This means that any methods that derive from research are
themselves liable to be discredited.

Another reason for the proliferation of methods is the diversity of
learning situations. People learn languages as children, as teens, and as

Principled Eclecticism | 123

adults. They learn them in their home country or in places where the language is spoken. They learn them intensively or part-time. They learn them in classrooms or in the street or by means of their mobile phones. They learn them for pleasure, for study, for work, for travel – or none of the above. Arguably, different methods cater better than others for different combinations of these variables.

Yet another reason for the emergence of so many methods might simply be fashion – or, put another way – ideology. Methods, it has been argued, are never disinterested: they embody particular views about the nature of mind, of language, of education, and of society – and the interconnections between all four. As beliefs and attitudes change, the need arises for new methods that enshrine these new beliefs. A case in point is the **Direct Method** (see chapter 3) which represented a shift from the view of language-as-cultural-object to one of language-as-transaction. Likewise, the **Communicative Approach** (see chapter 15) was the method that best reflected the drive towards the social reconstruction of post-war Europe.

Finally, methods have generally developed hand-in-hand with specific technologies, so as technologies evolve, so too do methods: 'gamification' (i.e. using features of computer game design to enhance educational software) is just one instance of this. Methods are also designed, it has to be admitted, for purely commercial reasons: a method, after all, is often a vehicle for the teaching materials, technologies and specialized training that can be marketed to support it. Certain branded methods are liable to this charge. Language teaching is big business, after all, and, like all businesses, it attracts its fair share of entrepreneurs.

How, then, is the teacher to choose?

Sometimes teachers have no choice: the institution or education authority that they work for tries to impose a method. Or, because they are at the outset of their career, some teachers prefer the security of a single 'teach-by-numbers' method. In either case, the challenge is to find what it is about the method that can be exploited to maximize learning, while (if possible) rejecting those aspects of it that are simply implausible.

Some teachers reject the method concept entirely, holding the view that methods are prescriptive, inflexible and insensitive to local conditions.

They may subscribe to what has been called the 'post-method condition' which, in turn, is associated with postmodernism and its rejection of the idea of universalist, objective knowledge and of 'one-size-fits-all' solutions to complex problems.

On the other hand, even postmodern teachers need to make decisions about syllabus, materials and classroom procedures. Chances are they will borrow from existing methods in ways that are consistent with their beliefs and their understanding of the local context. In that sense they are adopting what has been called 'principled eclecticism': 'They are in effect creating their own method by blending aspects of others in a principled manner' (Larsen-Freeman 2000). The idea is not new: as long ago as 1899, Henry Sweet (1899/1964) argued that 'a good method must, before all, be comprehensive and eclectic. It must be based on a thorough knowledge of the science of language'.

How does it work?

As this book has attempted to show, most methods have worked for someone, somewhere and at least some of the time. Hence, every method worth its name has something to offer the resourceful teacher. A number of allegedly effective classroom and self-study procedures have been mentioned in passing, including text memorization, reverse translation, 'shadowing', reading aloud, and contrastive analysis. But there is a difference between, on the one hand, simply stringing a sequence of borrowed techniques together in a somewhat random fashion, and, on the other, choosing those techniques which are consistent with a coherent theory of language learning. That is the difference, in short, between eclecticism and *principled* eclecticism. It is not the case, then, that 'anything goes'. At the very least, the principled teacher should be able to respond to the question 'Why did you do that?' with an answer that is grounded in some understanding of language, of language learning, and of the language learning context.

Does it work?

For some scholars, eclecticism – whether principled or not – has a bad name. H.H. Stern (1983), for example, writes: 'In my view, eclecticism does not recognize the fundamental weaknesses in the method concept as such, nor does it offer any guidance on what basis and by what principles aspects of different methods can be selected and combined'. In similar vein, Jack Richards (1990) argues that the teacher's focus should not be 'on the search for the best method, but rather on the circumstances and conditions under which more effective teaching and learning are accomplished'. He puts the case for a 'process-oriented methodology' in which teachers become investigators of their own classrooms. Such an approach, however, does not seem incompatible with principled eclecticism, if the principles that underpin the eclecticism are derived from the teacher's own exploratory practices.

What's in it for us?

In the end, all methods are eclectic, in the sense that they borrow from, build on, and recycle aspects of other methods. Our understanding of how and why this happens, and of how these same processes of appropriation and reconfiguration impact on our own teaching, is part of our ongoing professional development.

Advancing that understanding has been the purpose of this book. I hope that, in some small measure, this objective has been met.

Larsen-Freeman, D. (2000) *Techniques and Principles in Language Teaching (2nd Edition)*. Oxford: Oxford University Press.

Richards, J. (1990) *The Language Teaching Matrix*. Cambridge: Cambridge University Press.

Stern, H.H. (1983) *Fundamental Concepts of Language Teaching*. Oxford: Oxford University Press.

Sweet, H. (1899/1964) *The Practical Study of Languages*. Oxford: Oxford University Press.

Index

Printed in the United States
By Bookmasters